EDWARD III

ROYAL
SHAKESPEARE
COMPANY

EDWARD III

WILLIAM SHAKESPEARE

THIS EDITION PREPARED BY

ROGER WARREN

NICK HERN BOOKS

LONDON

www.nickhernbooks.co.uk

OTHER TITLES IN THIS SERIES

Jonson, Marston and Chapman
EASTWARD HO!

Philip Massinger
THE ROMAN ACTOR

John Fletcher
THE ISLAND PRINCESS

John Marston
THE MALCONTENT

———————————

This edition of *Edward III*
first published in Great Britain in 2002
as a paperback original by
Nick Hern Books Limited
14 Larden Road, London W3 7ST
in association with the
Royal Shakespeare Company

Cover design by RSC Graphics Department
Typeset by Country Setting, Kingsdown, Kent CT14 8ES
Printed by Biddles of Guildford

A CIP catalogue record for this book is available from
the British Library

ISBN 1 85459 694 2

THE ROYAL SHAKESPEARE COMPANY

The Royal Shakespeare Company is one of the world's best-known theatre ensembles.

The Company is widely regarded as one of the most important interpreters of Shakespeare and other dramatists. Today the RSC is at the leading edge of classical theatre, with an international reputation for artistic excellence, accessibility and high quality live performance.

Our mission at the Royal Shakespeare Company is to create outstanding theatre relevant to our times through the work of Shakespeare, other Renaissance dramatists, international and contemporary writers. Every year the Company plays to a million theatregoers at 2,000 performances, including over 50 weeks of UK and international touring.

We want to give as many people as possible, from all walks of life, a richer and fuller understanding and enjoyment of language and theatre. Through education and outreach programmes we continually strive to engage people with the experience of live performance.

The RSC's touchstone is the work of William Shakespeare. We are committed to presenting the widest range of Shakespeare's plays and demonstrating through performance the international and enduring appeal of his plays. We also want to inspire contemporary writers with the ambition of the Renaissance stage, presenting new plays alongside classical theatre.

The Company's roots in Stratford-upon-Avon stretch back to the nineteenth century. However, since the 1960s the RSC's work in Stratford has been complemented by a regular presence in London. But Stratford and London are only part of the story. Over 25 years of residency in the city of Newcastle upon Tyne have forged a profound link between RSC artists and audiences in the north east of England. Many of our productions also visit major regional theatres around Britain. And our annual regional tour sets up its own travelling auditorium in community centres, sport halls and schools in towns throughout the UK without access to professional theatre.

While the UK is the home of the Company, our audiences are global. The company regularly plays to enthusiastic theatregoers in other parts of Europe, across the United States, the Americas, Asia and Australasia. The RSC is proud of its relationships with partnering organisations in other countries, particularly in America.

Despite continual change, the RSC today is still at heart an ensemble Company. The continuation of this great tradition informs the work of all members of the Company. Directors, actors, dramatists and theatre practitioners all collaborate in the creation of the RSC's distinctive and unmistakable approach to theatre.

THE ROYAL SHAKESPEARE COMPANY

A PARTNERSHIP WITH THE RSC

The RSC is immensely grateful for the valuable support of its corporate sponsors and individual and charitable donors. Between them these groups provide up to £6m a year for the RSC and support a range of initiatives such as actor training, education workshops and access to our performances for all members of society.

The RSC is renowned throughout the world as one of the finest arts brands. A corporate partnership offers unique and creative opportunities, both nationally and internationally, and benefits from our long and distinguished record of maintaining and developing relationships. Reaching over one million theatregoers a year, our Corporate Partnership programme progresses from Corporate Membership to Business Partnership to Season Sponsor to Title Sponsor, and offers the following benefits: extensive crediting and association; prestigious corporate hospitality; marketing and promotional initiatives; corporate citizenship and business networking opportunities. Our commitment to education, new writing and access provides a diverse portfolio of projects which offer new and exciting ways to develop partnerships which are non-traditional and mutually beneficial.

As an individual you may wish to support the work of the RSC through membership of the RSC Patrons. For as little as £21 per month you can join a cast drawn from our audience and the worlds of theatre, film, politics and business. Alternatively, the gift of a legacy to the RSC would enable the company to maintain and increase new artistic and educational work with children and adults through the Acting and Education Funds.

For information about corporate partnership with the RSC, please contact Victoria Okotie, Head of Corporate Partnerships,
Barbican Theatre, London EC2Y 8BQ.
Tel: **020 7382 7132**.
e-mail: **victoria.okotie@rsc.org.uk**

For information about individual relationships with the RSC, please contact Graeme Williamson, Development Manager,
Royal Shakespeare Theatre, Waterside,
Stratford-upon-Avon CV37 6BB.
Tel: **01789 412661**.
e-mail: **graemew@rsc.org.uk**

For information about RSC Patrons, please contact Julia Read, Individual Giving Manager,
Royal Shakespeare Theatre, Waterside, Stratford-upon-Avon CV37 6BB.
Tel: **01789 412661**.
e-mail: **julia.read@rsc.org.uk**

You can visit our web site at
www.rsc.org.uk/development

RSC EDUCATION

The objective of the RSC Education Department is to enable as many people as possible, from all walks of life, to have easy access to the great works of Shakespeare, the Renaissance and the theatre.

To do this, we are building a team which supports the productions that the Company presents onstage for the general public, special interest groups and for education establishments of all kinds.

We are also planning to develop our contribution as a significant learning resource in the fields of Shakespeare, the Renaissance, classical and modern theatre, theatre arts and the RSC. This resource is made available in many different ways, including workshops, teachers' programmes, summer courses, a menu of activities offered to group members of the audience, pre- and post-show events as part of the Events programme, open days, tours of the theatre, community activities and youth programmes. The RSC Collections, moved into a new home, will be used to create new programmes of learning and an expanded exhibition schedule.

We are developing the educational component of our new web site to be launched this year. The RSC will make use of appropriate new technologies to disseminate its work in many different ways to its many audiences.

We can also use our knowledge of theatre techniques to help in other aspects of learning: classroom teaching techniques for subjects other than drama or English, including management and personnel issues.

Not all of these programmes are available all the time, and not all of them are yet in place. However, if you are interested in pursuing any of these options, the telephone numbers and e-mail addresses are as follows:

For information on general education activities contact the Education Administrator, Sarah Keevill, on **01789 403462**, or e-mail her on **sarah.keevill @rsc.org.uk.**

To find out about backstage tours, please contact our Tour Manager, Anne Tippett on **01789 403405**, or e-mail her on **theatre.tours@rsc.org.uk.**

STAY IN TOUCH

For up-to-date news on the RSC, our productions and education work visit the RSC's official web site: **www.rsc.org.uk**. Information on RSC performances is also available on Teletext

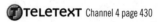 Channel 4 page 430

RSC MEMBERSHIP

Become an RSC Member and receive advance information and priority booking plus other exclusive benefits. Call our membership team on **01789 403440** for details of the various packages available, including UK membership, overseas, groups and education memberships. A free mailing list for those working in education is also available.

This production of *Edward III* was first performed by the Royal Shakespeare Company
in the Swan Theatre, Stratford-upon-Avon, on 10 April 2002.
The original cast was as follows:

David Acton	Earl of Salisbury
Paul Bentall	John Copland
Paul Bhattacharjee	Duke of Lorraine
Vincent Brimble	Earl of Derby
Antony Byrne	King David of Scotland
Wayne Cater	Lodowick
Caroline Faber	Countess of Salisbury
Jamie Glover	Edward, Prince of Wales
Sean Hannaway	Count of Artois
Sian Howard	Queen Philippa
Colin McCormack	Lord Audley
Keith Osborn	Mariner
Joshua Richards	Earl of Warwick
David Rintoul	King Edward III
Avin Shah	Prince Philip of France
Michael Thomas	King John of France
James Tucker	Prince Charles of France

Directed by	**Anthony Clark**
Designed by	**Patrick Connellan**
Lighting designed by	**Wayne Dowdeswell**
Movement by	**Ian Spink**
Fights by	**Terry King**
Sound designed by	**Martin Slavin**
Casting Director	**Carrie Hilton**
Associate Director	**Heather Davies**
Production Managers	**Stuart Gibbons and Mark Graham**
Costume Supervisor	**Janet Bench**
Dialect Coach	**Jeannette Nelson**
Company voice work by	**Andrew Wade and Jeannette Nelson**
Company Manager	**Jondon**

Stage Manager	**Leighton Vickers**
Deputy Stage Manager	**Amanda McCaffrey**
Assistant Stage Manager	**Christina Papaspyrou**

This production was sponsored in Stratford-upon-Avon by

BIRMINGHAM
INTERNATIONAL AIRPORT

Contents

Plays for a Money-Get, Mechanic Age

In his *An Expostulation with Inigo Jones,* Ben Jonson quarrels with Jones about the growing supremacy of scenery and stage effects over the spoken text, in the masques they produced together at court.

> Pack with your peddling poetry to the stage,
> This is a money-get, mechanic age.

The stage, unlike the court where the masques were held, was a place to go and use your eyes and your ears, a place where language had primacy, where you went to hear a play.

The stages of the Rose and the Globe needed no scenery, that would be conjured by words, words spoken by the actor standing in the centre of a circle of ears. The Swan Theatre in Stratford reproduces just such a relationship between actor and audience: vital, immediate and dangerous.

Since the Swan opened in 1986, we have done many plays from Shakespeare's time, all Jonson's major comedies (though none of his tragedies), all the major pays of Marlowe and Webster, as well as plays by Middleton and Ford, Kyd, Tourneur, Heywood and even Shirley and Broome. This season, I have chosen plays with which audiences are likely to be less familiar and which reflect something of the range of the drama of the period, from City Comedy to Revenge Tragedy and much in between.

I've included *Edward III,* recently canonized from the Shakespeare Apocrypha; *The Malcontent* by the unjustly neglected John Marston (this is his RSC debut); Massinger's magnificent *The Roman Actor* (Adrian Noble directed the only other Massinger play we've done, *A New Way to Pay Old Debts* at The Other Place in 1983); *Eastward Ho!,* a collaboration by Jonson, Marston and George Chapman; and finally, representing the popular genre of travel plays, a discovery, *The Island Princess* set in the Spice Islands and written by John Fletcher (who collaborated with Shakespeare on *Henry VIII or All Is True,* which I directed in the Swan in 1996).

This season is unusual not just because of the concentration on these lesser known plays from the repertoire, but because this is the first time we have explored these works with a dedicated ensemble company of 28 actors, who will perform all five plays in close repertoire. The Swan Theatre allows us to achieve this turnover very swiftly.

Though we have often had very large and elaborate scenery in the Swan, it works perfectly well without any; allowing all the flexibility and fluidity of Shakespeare's theatre. Basically very little set is needed for any of these plays and without much scenery of course we can achieve a much faster turnaround of plays and spend more time rehearsing in the space where we'll perform. So we have decided to work faster than usual in order to achieve a full repertoire by midsummer. And who knows, perhaps other things will be released by working all together at this pace, a different dynamic, a closer collaborative spirit? These days we are used to discussing character and motivation at length in rehearsal. Neither of these words would have been understood by an actor in Shakespeare's day. The text was the character. And as far as we can tell there was very little rehearsal at all. Nowadays we are used to letting things cook more slowly in rehearsal, so let's see what more of a stir-fry mentality can achieve!

It's a punishing schedule, but our workloads look light in comparison with the actors in Shakespeare's day. In the 1594-5 season at the Rose Theatre, according to Philip Henslowe's Diary, the Lord Admiral's Men performed 38 plays, 21 of which were new! It's a fascinating statistic and one which reflects the audience's appetite for drama in that 'money-get mechanic age'. Jonson's phrase could well describe our own time, and perhaps begins to suggest why the plays of Shakespeare and his contemporaries echo and resonate so profoundly with our own.

GREGORY DORAN

March 2002

INTRODUCTION

On 1 December 1595, the publisher Cuthbert Burby entered 'a book entitled Edward the Third and the Black Prince their wars with King John of France' on the Register of the Stationers' Company in London; he duly published *The Reign of King Edward III* the following year in a Quarto edition which forms the basis for the present performing text. Burby published a second Quarto in 1599, which corrects obvious errors but has no independent authority. The title-page of the First Quarto is uncommunicative: it mentions neither an author (or authors) nor the Elizabethan company who performed it, saying merely that 'it hath been sundry times played about the city of London'. There are no other references to the play during Shakespeare's lifetime.

Apart from an unreliable reference in a bookseller's catalogue of 1656, the first suggestion of Shakespearian authorship did not occur until 1760, when Edward Capell included *Edward III* in a volume preliminary to his complete edition of Shakespeare (1767–8) on the grounds that 'there was no known writer equal to such a play' and to allow his readers to form their own opinion about whether the play was by Shakespeare. Those who in the intervening centuries have responded to Capell's invitation fall into three categories: some flatly deny Shakespeare's authorship; some believe he wrote the whole play; probably the majority think the play collaborative, with Shakespeare primarily responsible for the episodes concerning Edward's attempt to seduce the Countess of Salisbury. This view arises from the belief that the Countess scenes are different in kind from the rest of the play. But since the play is in fact all of a piece, as will emerge from the discussion later on, there is no reason why it should not have been conceived and written by a single dramatist.

In its 2002 production, the RSC is presenting *Edward III* as a play by Shakespeare. Since there is no external evidence for the attribution, the case must depend upon internal evidence. This is of several kinds: the play's handling of its sources, its style, its structure, and the dramatist's attitude to the material. Despite its full title, the play understandably deals not with the entire length of Edward III's reign (1327–77) but with his conquest of France (1340–56), and with his violent passion for a 'Countess of Salisbury'. It is characteristic of Shakespeare to combine material from several different sources, and *Edward III* does this, deriving its basic narrative from Jean Froissart's *Chronicle* in Lord Berners' translation of 1523, but incorporating details from Holinshed's *Chronicles* (1587) for the military scenes and from William Painter's *Palace of*

Pleasure (1575) for the Countess ones. As in Shakespeare's histories, widely separated historical events, the battles of Sluys (1340), Crécy (1346), and Poitiers (1356), are brought together in a continuous dramatic sequence, and the first of these takes place after the Countess scenes rather than before, as in Froissart, so that the scenes of sexual intrigue are concluded before the military ones begin.

As far as style is concerned, it is not surprising that a play which shows the use of poetic language to further a dishonest love-suit should have verbal links with *Love's Labour's Lost* and Shakespeare's Sonnets, both much concerned with the appropriate ways for lovers to express truthfully what they feel. *Edward III* has in fact one line in common with Sonnet 94 – 'Lilies that fester smell far worse than weeds' – and it occurs in a speech that contains some other lines that seem particularly Shakespearian:

> An evil deed done by authority
> Is sin and subornation; deck an ape
> In tissue, and the beauty of the robe
> Adds but the greater scorn unto the beast.
>   (Scene 3, lines 443–6)

The play these lines evoke, however, is not one of the earlier works, but *Measure for Measure* (*c*. 1603):

>   man, proud man,
> Dressed in a little brief authority,
> Most ignorant of what he's most assured,
> His glassy essence, like an angry ape
> Plays such fantastic tricks before high heaven
> As makes the angels weep ...   (2.2.120–5)

The situations are, of course, similar: in each case a figure of authority (Edward, Angelo) abuses that authority in an attempt to corrupt a virtuous woman (the Countess, Isabella). Even so, the vivid phrasing and the pungent rhythm of the lines from *Edward III* seem not only Shakespearian, but *maturely* Shakespearian – so much so, indeed, that if they did not occur in a text published in 1596, one might suspect that they were a later addition.

Measure for Measure is anticipated in another striking speech. Outnumbered by the French before the battle of Poitiers, the Black Prince asks his mentor Audley for counsel in 'this perilous time'. Audley replies:

> To die is all as common as to live;
> The one in choice the other holds in chase,

> For from the instant we begin to live,
> We do pursue and hunt the time to die. ...
> If then we hunt for death, why do we fear it?
> If we fear it, why do we follow it?
> If we do follow it, how can we shun it?
>   (Scene 12, lines 133–42)

The tone here is close to the Duke's in *Measure for Measure* as he counsels Claudio, another youth faced with death, to accept it –

> Merely thou art death's fool,
> For him thou labour'st by thy flight to shun,
> And yet runn'st toward him still –

and to Claudio's reply:

> To sue to live, I find I seek to die,
> And seeking death, find life. Let it come on.
>   (3.1.11–43)

Edward III connects with Shakespeare's work in matters of structure as well as language. In dramatizing 'Edward the Third and the Black Prince their wars with King John of France', the play shows events on the world stage in terms of personalities, as often in Shakespeare's undisputed work. This is why the Countess scenes are so important, and so integral. Far from being disconnected elements indicative of divided authorship, Edward's obsession with the Countess and his conquest of France are inter-related. Edward himself puts it concisely:

> Shall the large limit of fair Brittany
> By me be overthrown, and shall I not
> Master this little mansion of myself?
>   (Scene 4, lines 92–4)

It is the sight of his son, the Black Prince, that prompts this self-analysis; and Edward's relationship with these two characters governs the structure of the play: he is set against the Countess in the first half, against his son in the second. If he learns to 'master' himself in the Countess episode, it is a lesson insecurely learnt, since he still needs another woman, his wife Queen Philippa, to persuade him to temper his fury against the citizens of Calais in the final scene. As for his relationship with his son, Edward's military ruthlessness, as in his refusal to let anyone help his son at Crécy, is juxtaposed with the chivalric ritual of the Black Prince's formal arming; later, the Prince's genuine heroism at Poitiers, indignantly refusing the French heralds' temptations to yield despite the odds, is contrasted with his father's threatened brutality to Calais; and the Prince's willingness to ask for advice from Audley in the scene already quoted perhaps hints at a psychological need that his father may not be able to supply.

This principal structural balance is supported by another. It concerns the keeping or breaking of oaths. In the first half of the play, Edward attempts to use oaths extorted from the Countess and her father Warwick in order to force the Countess to yield to him. The seriousness of oath-taking is spelt out:

King   What wilt thou say to one that breaks an oath?

Warwick   That he hath broke his faith with God and man
              And from them both stands excommunicate.
              (Scene 3, lines 331–3)

In the second half, much is made of an episode in which oaths are taken by the Dauphin and his friend Villiers to guarantee safe conduct to one of the English lords. The French king attempts unsuccessfully to force them to break their oaths. The dramatist departs from the chronicle source here in order to make the English lord concerned the Earl of Salisbury – presumably the Countess's husband. In this way, wife and husband are put into parallel dangerous situations, both involving the keeping or breaking of oaths, an excellent example of the tight organization of the play and how it binds the two halves, which might be called the sexual and the military, together. The seriousness of oaths is a recurrent Shakespearian preoccupation. It occurs frequently in the conflicting loyalties of the histories, notably in *2 Henry VI* where another Earl of Salisbury finds it necessary, and embarrassing, to justify breaking his oath to Henry VI in supporting the house of York. It is even more central to *Love's Labour's Lost*: if the lords can so easily break the oaths to study that they took at the start of the play, how can the ladies take seriously their vows of love? The entire action of *Love's Labour's Lost*, and especially its sombre ending, hinges on the binding quality of the initial oath.

At first sight, *Edward III* seems formal, heraldic even. But a glance at its main source puts that into perspective. Froissart's tone is chivalric, very close to that of Malory's *Morte D'Arthur* (published in 1485), and the English used in Lord Berners' translation emphasizes this connection. The world of *Edward III* is much tougher, and allows glimpses of something darker behind both language and events. Froissart drew on an earlier French writer, Jean le Bel. The Countess in the play seems to be an amalgam of three separate women, one of whom, called by le Bel 'Alice, Countess of Salisbury', rejected Edward's advances; so 'he raped her so savagely that never was a woman so badly treated; and he left her lying there all battered about, bleeding from the nose and the mouth and elsewhere. ... Then he left the next day without saying a word'. But if le Bel's version had a factual basis, it probably involved, not a 'Countess of Salisbury', but Alice, Lady Montagu, who was the victim of a particularly ugly episode: she was beaten to death by her husband in 1351, and Edward would not allow him to be prosecuted for it. Froissart deliberately softened le Bel's account, not surprisingly: he was both secretary to Edward's wife Queen Philippa, and the court chronicler. Behind Froissart's elegant, courtly version lies something much more disturbing, and although the dramatist could not have known le Bel's account since it disappeared between the fourteenth and nineteenth centuries, he instinctively caught some of its extremity and outrage in what Edward himself calls the 'violent extremes' of his desires and in the personal tensions between the King and the Countess.

As for the political tensions, the play deals with the King's triumphant conquest of France, as *Henry V* does later. But *Henry V*, of course, provides an ambivalent view of this. The Chorus presents the idealized Harry of tradition; the rest of the play probes searchingly into character and situation, as when the initial claim to France is set within a context of ecclesiastical self-interest, or when, at Agincourt, the King orders the killing of the French prisoners because they are a military encumbrance. *Edward III* likewise asserts yet subverts the chivalric ideal: it makes no bones about the savagery that accompanies the conquests, as reported by the French refugees, or when Edward threatens Calais.

Capell in 1760 invited the public to form their own opinion about the authorship question by reading 'what is now before' them. Audiences, however, have been given almost no chance to do this. *Edward III* has never before been staged at Stratford, and very rarely anywhere else: in Los Angeles (1986), Theatr Clwyd (1987), and Cologne (1999). The 2002 RSC production at the Swan therefore offers audiences an opportunity to decide for themselves, and to experience a play much discussed but seldom to be found where it belongs: in the theatre.

THIS EDITION

This performing text closely follows Quarto 1, incorporating corrections from Quarto 2 but keeping emendations to a minimum, and using the original stage directions as far as possible. It uses lighter punctuation than strictly grammatical usage would require, so as to preserve the shape and rhythm of the verse lines and to avoid unnecessary obstacles to their speaking. I am very grateful to Richard Proudfoot and Nicola Bennett for allowing me to base this text on the type facsimile of Quarto 1 which they have prepared in connection with their forthcoming Arden edition of *Edward III*, and to Angie Kendall for her extensive help in preparing this performing text.

ROGER WARRREN

CHARACTERS

King Edward III
Edward 'the Black Prince', his son
Robert of Artois, a French lord
Duke of Lorraine, ambassador from France
Lord Audley
Earl of Warwick
Earl of Derby
Sir William Montague
The Countess of Salisbury
King David of Scotland
Sir William Douglas
Two Scots messengers
Lodowick, King Edward's secretary
King John of France
Charles Duke of Normandy, the Dauphin
Philip, King John's younger son
King of Bohemia
Polish captain
French mariner
Three Frenchmen
Two French citizens
Frenchwoman
Gobin de Grace
Four English heralds
Montfort, a French lord
Earl of Salisbury
Villiers, a French lord
Six poor Frenchmen from Calais
Lord Percy
Captain of Calais
Three French heralds
French captain
Two squires
Six citizens of Calais
Queen Philippe, King Edward's wife
John Copland, an English squire

EDWARD III

SCENE ONE

Enter King Edward, Derby, Prince Edward, Audley,
Warwick, and Artois

King   Robert of Artois, banished though thou be
From France thy native country, yet with us
Thou shalt retain as great a signory,
For we create thee Earl of Richmond here.
And now go forwards with our pedigree: 5
Who next succeeded Philip le Beau?

Artois   Three sons of his, which all successively
Did sit upon their father's regal throne,
Yet died and left no issue of their loins.

King   But was my mother sister unto those?   10

Artois   She was, my lord, and only Isabel
Was all the daughters that this Philip had,
Whom afterward your father took to wife,
And from the fragrant garden of her womb
Your gracious self, the flower of Europe's hope,   15
Derivèd is inheritor to France.
But note the rancour of rebellious minds:
When thus the lineage of le Beau was out,
The French obscured your mother's privilege,
And though she were the next of blood, proclaimed   20
John of the house of Valois now their king.
The reason was, they say the realm of France,
Replete with princes of great parentage,
Ought not admit a governor to rule
Except he be descended of the male,   25
And that's the special ground of their contempt
Wherewith they study to exclude your grace.

| King | But they shall find that forgèd ground of theirs |
| | To be but dusty heaps of brittle sand. |

Artois	Perhaps it will be thought a heinous thing	30
	That I a Frenchman should discover this,
	But heaven I call to record of my vows,
	It is not hate nor any private wrong,
	But love unto my country and the right,
	Provokes my tongue thus lavish in report.	35
	You are the lineal watchman of our peace,
	And John of Valois indirectly climbs.
	What then should subjects but embrace their king?
	Ah, wherein may our duty more be seen,
	Than striving to rebate a tyrant's pride,	40
	And place the true shepherd of our commonwealth?

King	This counsel, Artois, like to fruitful showers,
	Hath added growth unto my dignity,
	And by the fiery vigour of thy words
	Hot courage is engendered in my breast,	45
	Which heretofore was racked in ignorance,
	But now doth mount with golden wings of fame,
	And will approve fair Isabel's descent,
	Able to yoke their stubborn necks with steel
	That spurn against my sovereignty in France.	50

Sound a horn

A messenger, Lord Audley, know from whence.

Enter Lorraine, a messenger

| Audley | The Duke of Lorraine, having crossed the seas, |
| | Entreats he may have conference with your highness. |

| King | Admit him lords, that we may hear the news. |
| | Say, Duke of Lorraine, wherefore art thou come. | 55 |

| Lorraine | The most renownèd prince, King John of France, |
| | Doth greet thee Edward, and by me commands, |

That for so much as by his liberal gift
The Guyenne dukedom is entailed to thee,
Thou do him lowly homage for the same.   60
And for that purpose here I summon thee
Repair to France within these forty days,
That there according as the custom is,
Thou mayst be sworn true liegeman to our king,
Or else thy title in that province dies,   65
And he himself will repossess the place.

King   See how occasion laughs me in the face,
              No sooner minded to prepare for France,
              But straight I am invited, nay with threats
              Upon a penalty enjoined to come.   70
              'Twere but a childish part to say him nay.
              Lorraine, return this answer to thy lord:
              I mean to visit him as he requests,
              But how? Not servilely disposed to bend,
              But like a conquerer to make him bow.   75
              His lame unpolished shifts are come to light,
              And truth hath pulled the visor from his face,
              That set a gloss upon his arrogance.
              Dare he command a fealty in me?
              Tell him the crown that he usurps is mine, 80
              And where he sets his foot he ought to kneel.
              'Tis not a petty dukedom that I claim,
              But all the whole dominions of the realm,
              Which if with grudging he refuse to yield,
              I'll take away those borrowed plumes of his 85
              And send him naked to the wilderness.

Lorraine   Then Edward, here in spite of all thy lords,
              I do pronounce defiance to thy face.

Prince   Defiance, Frenchman? We rebound it back,
              Even to the bottom of thy master's throat; 90
              And be it spoke with reverence of the King

My gracious father and these other lords,
I hold thy message but as scurrilous,
And him that sent thee like the lazy drone
Crept up by stealth unto the eagle's nest,   95
From whence we'll shake him with so rough a storm
As others shall be warnèd by his harm.

Warwick   Bid him leave off the lion's case he wears,
Lest meeting with the lion in the field,
He chance to tear him piecemeal for his pride.   100

Artois   The soundest counsel I can give his grace
Is to surrender ere he be constrained.
A voluntary mischief hath less scorn
Than when reproach with violence is borne.

Lorraine   Degenerate traitor, viper to the place   105
Where thou was fostered in thine infancy,
Bear'st thou a part in this conspiracy?

                        He draws his sword

King   Lorraine, behold the sharpness of this steel (*draws*).
Fervent desire that sits against my heart
Is far more thorny pricking than this blade,   110
That with the nightingale I shall be scarred,
As oft as I dispose myself to rest,
Until my colours be displayed in France.
This is thy final answer, so be gone.

Lorraine   It is not that nor any English brave,   115
Afflicts me so, as doth his poisoned view,
That is most false, should most of all be true.   *Exit*

King   Now lords, our fleeting barque is under sail,
Our gage is thrown, and war is soon begun,
But not so quickly brought unto an end.   120

                        Enter Montague

But wherefore comes Sir William Montague?
How stands the league between the Scot and us?

Montague   Cracked and dissevered, my renownèd lord:
The treacherous King no sooner was informed
Of your withdrawing of your army back,   125
But straight forgetting of his former oath,
He made invasion on the bordering towns:
Berwick is won, Newcastle spoiled and lost,
And now the tyrant hath begirt with siege
The Castle of Roxborough, where enclosed   130
The Countess Salisbury is like to perish.

King   That is thy daughter, Warwick, is it not,
Whose husband hath in Bretagne served so long,
About the planting of Lord Montfort there?

Warwick   It is my lord.   135

King   Ignoble David, hast thou none to grieve
But silly ladies with thy threat'ning arms?
But I will make you shrink your snaily horns.
First therefore Audley, this shall be thy charge:
Go levy footmen for our wars in France;   140
And Ned, take muster of our men at arms,
In every shire elect a several band,
Let them be soldiers of a lusty spirit,
Such as dread nothing but dishonour's blot.
Be wary therefore, since we do commence   145
A famous war, and with so mighty a nation.
Derby, be thou ambassador for us
Unto our father-in-law, the Earl of Hainault:
Make him acquainted with our enterprise,
And likewise will him with our own allies   150
That are in Flanders to solicit too
The Emperor of Almagne in our name.
Myself, whilst you are jointly thus employed,
Will with these forces that I have at hand

March and once more repulse the traitorous Scot.   155
But sirs, be resolute, we shall have wars
On every side; and Ned, thou must begin
Now to forget thy study and thy books,
And ure thy shoulders to an armour's weight.

Prince   As cheerful sounding to my youthful spleen   160
This tumult is of war's increasing broils,
As at the coronation of a king
The joyful clamours of the people are,
When *Ave Caesar* they pronounce aloud.
Within this school of honour I shall learn   165
Either to sacrifice my foes to death
Or in a rightful quarrel spend my breath.
Then cheerfully forward, each a several way,
In great affairs 'tis naught to use delay.

Exeunt

SCENE TWO

Enter the Countess

Countess   Alas, how much in vain my poor eyes gaze
For succour that my sovereign should send.
Ah cousin Montague, I fear thou wants
The lively spirit sharply to solicit
With vehement suit the king in my behalf.   5
Thou dost not tell him what a grief it is
To be the scornful captive to a Scot,
Either to be wooed with broad untunèd oaths,
Or forced by rough insulting barbarism;
Thou dost not tell him if he here prevail,   10
How much they will deride us in the north,
And in their wild uncivil skipping jigs,
Bray forth their conquest and our overthrow,
Even in the barren, bleak and fruitless air.

Enter King David, Douglas, and Lorraine

I must withdraw, the everlasting foe   15
Comes to the wall; I'll closely step aside,
And list their babble, blunt and full of pride.

King David My lord of Lorraine, to our brother of France
Commend us as the man in Christendom
That we most reverence and entirely love.   20
Touching your embassage, return and say
That we with England will not enter parley,
Nor never make fair weather or take truce,
But burn their neighbour towns, and so persist
With eager rods beyond their city York;   25
And never shall our bonny riders rest,

Nor rusting canker have the time to eat
Their light-borne snaffles, nor their nimble spurs,
Nor lay aside their jacks of gimmaled mail,
Nor hang their staves of grainèd Scottish ash,   30
In peaceful wise upon their city walls,
Nor from their buttoned tawny leathern belts
Dismiss their biting whinyards, till your king
Cry out 'Enough, spare England now for pity'.
Farewell, and tell him that you leave us here   35
Before this castle, say you came from us
Even when we had that yielded to our hands.

Lorraine   I take my leave and fairly will return
               Your acceptable greeting to my king.   *Exit*

King David   Now Douglas, to our former task again,   40
               For the division of this certain spoil.

Douglas   My liege, I crave the lady and no more.

King David   Nay soft ye sir, first I must make my choice,
               And first I do bespeak her for myself.

Douglas   Why then my liege, let me enjoy her jewels.   45

King David   Those are her own, still liable to her,
               And who inherits her, hath those withal.

                Enter a Scot, a messenger, in haste

Messenger   My liege, as we were pricking on the hills
               To fetch in booty, marching hitherward
               We might descry a mighty host of men.   50
               The sun reflecting on the armour showed
               A field of plate, a wood of pikes advanced.
               Bethink your highness speedily herein,
               An easy march within four hours will bring
               The hindmost rank unto this place, my liege.   55

King David   Dislodge, dislodge, it is the king of England.

Douglas   Jemmy my man, saddle my bonny black.

King David Mean'st thou to fight, Douglas? We are too weak.

Douglas   I know it well my liege, and therefore fly.

Countess   My lords of Scotland, will ye stay and drink?   60

King David She mocks at us Douglas, I cannot endure it.

Countess   Say good my lord, which is he must have the lady,
              And which her jewels? I am sure my lords,
              Ye will not hence till you have shared the spoils.

King David She heard the messenger, and heard our talk,
              And now that comfort makes her scorn at us.   65

                    Enter another messenger

2 Messenger Arm, my good lord, O we are all surprised.

Countess   After the French ambassador, my liege,
              And tell him that you dare not ride to York;
              Excuse it that your bonny horse is lame.   70

King David She heard that too, intolerable grief:
              Woman farewell; although I do not stay –   *Exeunt Scots*

Countess   'Tis not for fear, and yet you run away.
              O happy comfort, welcome to our house.
              The confident and boist'rous boasting Scot,   75
              That swore before my walls they would not back
              For all the armèd power of this land,
              With faceless fear that ever turns his back,
              Turned hence against the blasting north-east wind
              Upon the bare report and name of arms.   80

                        Enter Montague

              O summer's day, see where my cousin comes.

Montague   How fares my aunt? We are not Scots,
              Why do you shut your gates against your friends?

Countess	Well may I give a welcome, cousin, to thee,
	For thou com'st well to chase my foes from hence. 85
Montague	The king himself is come in person hither.
	Dear aunt, descend and 'gratulate his highness.
Countess	How may I entertain his majesty,
	To show my duty, and his dignity? [*Exit above*]

Enter King Edward, Warwick, Artois, with others

King	What, are the stealing foxes fled and gone 90
	Before we could uncouple at their heels?
Warwick	They are, my liege, but with a cheerful cry,
	Hot hounds and hardy chase them at the heels.

Enter the Countess

King	This is the Countess, Warwick, is it not?
Warwick	Even she, my liege, whose beauty tyrants fear, 95
	As a May blossom with pernicious winds
	Hath sullied, withered, overcast, and done.
King	Hath she been fairer, Warwick, than she is?
Warwick	My gracious King, fair is she not at all,
	If that herself were by to stain herself, 100
	As I have seen her when she was herself.
King	What strange enchantment lurked in those her eyes
	When they excelled this excellence they have,
	That now her dim decline hath power to draw
	My subject eyes from piercing majesty, 105
	To gaze on her with doting admiration?
Countess	In duty lower than the ground I kneel,
	And for my dull knees bow my feeling heart
	To witness my obedience to your highness,
	With many millions of a subject's thanks 110
	For this your royal presence, whose approach
	Hath driven war and danger from my gate.

| King | Lady stand up, I come to bring thee peace, |
| | However thereby I have purchased war. |

| Countess | No war to you my liege, the Scots are gone,   115 |
| | And gallop home toward Scotland with their hate. |

| King | Lest yielding here I pine in shameful love, |
| | Come we'll pursue the Scots. – Artois away. |

Countess	A little while, my gracious sovereign, stay,
	And let the power of a mighty king 120
	Honour our roof; my husband in the wars
	When he shall hear it will triumph for joy.
	Then dear my liege, now niggard not thy state;
	Being at the wall, enter our homely gate.

| King | Pardon me Countess, I will come no near'r,   125 |
| | I dreamed tonight of treason and I fear. |

| Countess | Far from this place let ugly treason lie. |

King	No farther off than her conspiring eye,
	Which shoots infected poison in my heart,
	Beyond repulse of wit or cure of art. 130
	Now in the sun alone it doth not lie,
	With light to take light from a mortal eye;
	For here two day-stars that mine eyes would see,
	More than the sun steals mine own light from me.
	Contemplative desire, desire to be 135
	In contemplation that may master thee. –
	Warwick, Artois, to horse and let's away.

| Countess | What might I speak to make my sovereign stay? |

| King | What needs a tongue to such a speaking eye, |
| | That more persuades than winning oratory?   140 |

Countess	Let not thy presence like the April sun
	Flatter our earth, and suddenly be done.
	More happy do not make our outward wall

Than thou wilt grace our inner house withal.
Our house, my liege, is like a country swain,   145
Whose habit rude and manners blunt and plain
Presageth naught, yet inly beautified
With bounty's riches and fair hidden pride:
For where the golden ore doth buried lie,
The ground, undecked with nature's tapestry,   150
Seems barren, sere, unfertile, fruitless, dry;
And where the upper turf of earth doth boast
His pride, perfumes, and parti-coloured cost,
Delve there, and find this issue and their pride
To spring from ordure and corruption's side.   155
But to make up my all too long compare,
These raggèd walls no testimony are
What is within, but like a cloak doth hide
From weather's waste the undergarnished pride:
More gracious than my terms can, let thee be;   160
Entreat thyself to stay a while with me.

King   As wise as fair, what fond fit can be heard,
When wisdom keeps the gate as beauty's guard? –
Countess, albeit my business urgeth me,
It shall attend, while I attend on thee.   165
Come on my lords, here will I host tonight.   *Exeunt*

SCENE THREE

Enter Lodowick

Lodowick   I might perceive his eye in her eye lost,
His ear to drink her sweet tongue's utterance,
And changing passions like inconstant clouds,
That rack upon the carriage of the winds,
Increase and die in his disturbèd cheeks.   5
Lo, when she blushed, even then did he look pale,
As if her cheeks by some enchanted power
Attracted had the cherry blood from his;
Anon, with reverent fear when she grew pale,
His cheek put on their scarlet ornaments,   10
But no more like her oriental red
Than brick to coral, or live things to dead.
Why did he then thus counterfeit her looks?
If she did blush, 'twas tender modest shame,
Being in the sacred presence of a king;   15
If he did blush, 'twas red immodest shame,
To vail his eyes amiss, being a king.
If she looked pale, 'twas silly woman's fear,
To bear herself in presence of a king;
If he looked pale, it was with guilty fear,   20
To dote amiss, being a mighty king.
Then Scottish wars farewell, I fear 'twill prove
A ling'ring English siege of peevish love.
Here comes his highness walking all alone.

Enter King Edward

King   She is grown more fairer far since I came hither,   25
Her voice more silver every word than other,
Her wit more fluent; what a strange discourse

Unfolded she of David and his Scots:
'Even thus', quoth she, 'he spake', and then spoke broad,
With epithets and accents of the Scot,   30
But somewhat better than the Scot could speak,
'And thus', quoth she, and answered then herself,
For who could speak like her? But she herself
Breathes from the wall an angel's note from heaven
Of sweet defiance to her barbarous foes.   35
When she would talk of peace methinks her tongue
Commanded war to prison; when of war,
It wakened Caesar from his Roman grave,
To hear war beautified by her discourse.
Wisdom is foolishness but in her tongue,   40
Beauty a slander but in her fair face,
There is no summer but in her cheerful looks,
Nor frosty winter but in her disdain.
I cannot blame the Scots that did besiege her,
For she is all the treasure of our land,   45
But call them cowards that they ran away,
Having so rich and fair a cause to stay.
Art thou there, Lod'wick? Give me ink and paper.

Lodowick	I will my liege.

King	And bid the lords hold on their play at chess,	50
	For we will walk and meditate alone.	

Lodowick	I will my sovereign.	*Exit*

King	This fellow is well read in poetry,
	And hath a lusty and persuasive spirit:

I will acquaint him with my passion,   55
Which he shall shadow with a veil of lawn,
Through which the queen of beauty's queen shall see
Herself the ground of my infirmity.

Enter Lodowick

King	Hast thou pen, ink, and paper ready, Lodowick?

Lodowick   Ready my liege.   60

King   Then in the summer arbour sit by me,
Make it our counsel house or cabinet:
Since green our thoughts, green be the conventicle,
Where we will ease us by disburd'ning them.
Now Lod'wick, invocate some golden muse   65
To bring thee hither an enchanted pen,
That may for sighs set down true sighs indeed,
Talking of grief, to make thee ready groan,
And when thou writ'st of tears, encouch the word
Before and after with such sweet laments,   70
That it may raise drops in a Tartar's eye,
And make a flint-heart Scythian pitiful;
For so much moving hath a poet's pen.
Then if thou be a poet move thou so,
And be enrichèd by thy sovereign's love: 75
For if the touch of sweet concordant strings
Could force attendance in the ears of hell,
How much more shall the strains of poets' wit
Beguile and ravish soft and human minds!

Lodowick   To whom, my lord, shall I direct my style?   80

King   To one that shames the fair and sots the wise,
Whose body is an abstract or a brief,
Contains each general virtue in the world.
'Better than beautiful' thou must begin,
Devise for fair a fairer word than fair,   85
And every ornament that thou wouldst praise,
Fly it a pitch above the soar of praise.
For flattery fear thou not to be convicted,
For were thy admiration ten times more,
Ten times ten thousand more the worth exceeds   90
Of that thou art to praise, thy praise's worth.
Begin, I will to contemplate the while.
Forget not to set down how passionate,

How heart-sick and how full of languishment
Her beauty makes me.

Lodowick   Write I to a woman?   95

King   What beauty else could triumph over me,
Or who but women do our love-lays greet?
What, think'st thou I did bid thee praise a horse?

Lodowick   Of what condition or estate she is
'Twere requisite that I should know, my lord.   100

King   Of such estate, that hers is as a throne,
And my estate the footstool where she treads;
Then mayst thou judge what her condition is
By the proportion of her mightiness.
Write on while I peruse her in my thoughts.   105
Her voice to music or the nightingale –
To music every summer-leaping swain
Compares his sunburnt lover when she speaks,
And why should I speak of the nightingale?
The nightingale sings of adulterate wrong,   110
And that compared is too satirical,
For sin though sin would not be so esteemed,
But rather virtue sin, sin virtue deemed.
Her hair far softer then the silkworm's twist,
Like to a flattering glass doth make more fair   115
The yellow amber – 'like a flattering glass'
Comes in too soon; for writing of her eyes,
I'll say that like a glass they catch the sun,
And thence the hot reflection doth rebound
Against my breast and burns my heart within.   120
Ah what a world of descant makes my soul
Upon this voluntary ground of love.
Come Lod'wick, hast thou turned thy ink to gold?
If not, write but in letters capital
My mistress' name, and it will gild thy paper.   125
Read, Lod'wick, read.

Fill thou the empty hollows of mine ears
With the sweet hearing of thy poetry.

Lodowick   I have not to a period brought her praise.

King   Her praise is as my love, both infinite,   130
Which apprehend such violent extremes
That they disdain an ending period.
Her beauty hath no match but my affection,
Hers more than most, mine most, and more than more,
Hers more to praise than tell the sea by drops,   135
Nay more than drop the massy earth by sands,
And sand by sand, print them in memory.
Then wherefore talk'st thou of a period
To that which craves unended admiration?
Read, let us hear.   140

Lodowick   'More fair and chaste than is the queen of shades.'

King   That line hath two faults, gross and palpable.
Compar'st thou her to the pale queen of night,
Who being set in dark seems therefore light?
What, is she when the sun lifts up his head,   145
But like a fading taper dim and dead?
My love shall brave the eye of heaven at noon,
And being unmasked, outshine the golden sun.

Lodowick   What is the other fault, my sovereign lord?

King   Read o'er the line again.

Lodowick   'More fair and chaste' –   150

King   I did not bid thee talk of chastity,
To ransack so the treasure of her mind,
For I had rather have her chased than chaste.
Out with the moon line, I will none of it,
And let me have her likened to the sun.   155
Say she hath thrice more splendour than the sun,
That her perfections emulates the sun,

That she breeds sweets as plenteous as the sun,
That she doth thaw cold winter like the sun,
That she doth cheer fresh summer like the sun,   160
That she doth dazzle gazers like the sun,
And in this application to the sun,
Bid her be free and general as the sun,
Who smiles upon the basest weed that grows
As lovingly as on the fragrant rose.   165
Let's see what follows that same moonlight line.

Lodowick   'More fair and chaste than is the queen of shades,
            More bold in constancy' –

King   In constancy than who?

Lodowick   'Than Judith was.'

King   O monstrous line! Put in the next a sword   170
            And I shall woo her to cut off my head.
            Blot, blot, good Lod'wick, let us hear the next.

Lodowick   There's all that yet is done.

King   I thank thee then, thou hast done little ill,
            But what is done is passing passing ill.   175
            No, let the captain talk of boist'rous war,
            The prisoner of immurèd dark constraint,
            The sick man best sets down the pangs of death,
            The man that starves the sweetness of a feast,
            The frozen soul the benefit of fire,   180
            And every grief his happy opposite.
            Love cannot sound well but in lovers' tongues.
            Give me the pen and paper, I will write.

                        Enter the Countess

            But soft, here comes the treasurer of my spirit.
            Lod'wick, thou know'st not how to draw a battle. 185
            These wings, these flankers, and these squadrons,
            Argue in thee defective discipline.
            Thou shouldst have placed this here, this other here.

Countess	Pardon my boldness, my thrice gracious lords.	
	Let my intrusion here be called my duty,	190
	That comes to see my sovereign how he fares.	

King   Go draw the same, I tell thee in what form.

Lodowick I go.   *Exit*

Countess Sorry I am to see my liege so sad.
          What may thy subject do to drive from thee   195
          Thy gloomy consort, sullen melancholy?

King   Ah lady, I am blunt and cannot strew
          The flowers of solace in a ground of shame.
          Since I came hither, Countess, I am wronged.

Countess Now God forbid that any in my house   200
          Should think my sovereign wrong! Thrice gentle King,
          Acquaint me with thy cause of discontent.

King   How near then shall I be to remedy?

Countess As near, my liege, as all my woman's power
          Can pawn itself to buy thy remedy.   205

King   If thou speak'st true then have I my redress.
          Engage thy power to redeem my joys,
          And I am joyful, Countess, else I die.

Countess I will, my liege.

King   Swear, Countess, that thou wilt.

Countess By heaven I will.   210

King   Then take thyself a little way aside,
          And tell thyself a king doth dote on thee;
          Say that within thy power doth lie
          To make him happy, and that thou hast sworn
          To give him all the joy within thy power.   215
          Do this and tell me when I shall be happy.

Countess	All this is done, my thrice dread sovereign.
	That power of love that I have power to give
	Thou hast with all devout obedience.
	Employ me how thou wilt in proof thereof. 220
King	Thou hear'st me say that I do dote on thee.
Countess	If on my beauty, take it if thou canst;
	Though little, I do prize it ten times less.
	If on my virtue, take it if thou canst,
	For virtue's store by giving doth augment. 225
	Be it on what it will that I can give,
	An thou canst take away, inherit it.
King	It is thy beauty that I would enjoy.
Countess	O were it painted I would wipe it off,
	And dispossess myself to give it thee; 230
	But sovereign, it is soldered to my life.
	Take one and both, for like an humble shadow,
	It haunts the sunshine of my summer's life.
King	But thou mayst lend it me to sport withal.
Countess	As easy may my intellectual soul 235
	Be lent away and yet my body live,
	As lend my body, palace to my soul,
	Away from her and yet retain my soul.
	My body is her bower, her court, her abbey,
	And she an angel pure, divine, unspotted. 240
	If I should leave her house, my lord, to thee,
	I kill my poor soul and my poor soul me.
King	Didst thou not swear to give me what I would?
Countess	I did, my liege, so what you would I could.
King	I wish no more of thee than thou mayst give, 245
	Nor beg I do not but I rather buy:
	That is thy love, and for that love of thine,
	In rich exchange I tender to thee mine.

Countess	But that your lips were sacred, my lord,
	You would profane the holy name of love. 250
	That love you offer me you cannot give,
	For Caesar owes that tribute to his queen;
	That love you beg of me I cannot give,
	For Sarah owes that duty to her lord.
	He that doth clip or counterfeit your stamp 255
	Shall die, my lord; and will your sacred self
	Commit high treason against the king of heaven,
	To stamp his image in forbidden metal,
	Forgetting your allegiance and your oath?
	In violating marriage' sacred law, 260
	You break a greater honour than yourself.
	To be a king is of a younger house,
	Than to be married: your progenitor,
	Sole reigning Adam on the universe,
	By God was honoured for a married man, 265
	But not by him anointed for a king.
	It is a penalty to break your statutes,
	Though not enacted with your highness' hand;
	How much more to infringe the holy act
	Made by the mouth of God, sealed with his hand? 270
	I know my sovereign in my husband's love,
	Who now doth loyal service in his wars,
	Doth but to try the wife of Salisbury,
	Whether she will hear a wanton's tale or no.
	Lest being therein guilty by my stay, 275
	From that, not from my liege, I turn away. *Exit*
King	Whether is her beauty by her words divine,
	Or are her words sweet chaplains to her beauty?
	Like as the wind doth beautify a sail,
	And as a sail becomes the unseen wind, 280
	So do her words her beauty, beauty words.
	O that I were a honey-gathering bee,
	To bear the comb of virtue from this flower,

And not a poison-sucking envious spider,
To turn the juice I take to deadly venom!   285
Religion is austere and beauty gentle,
Too strict a guardian for so fair a ward.
O that she were as is the air to me!
Why so she is, for when I would embrace her,
This do I, and catch nothing but myself.   290
I must enjoy her, for I cannot beat
With reason and reproof fond love away.

Enter Warwick

Here comes her father, I will work with him
To bear my colours in this field of love.

Warwick	How is it that my sovereign is so sad?	295
	May I with pardon know your highness' grief,	
	And that my old endeavour will remove it,	
	It shall not cumber long your majesty.	
King	A kind and voluntary gift thou profferest,	
	That I was forward to have begged of thee.	300
	But O thou world, great nurse of flattery,	
	Why dost thou tip men's tongues with golden words,	
	And peise their deeds with weight of heavy lead,	
	That fair performance cannot follow promise?	
	O that a man might hold the heart's close book,	305
	And choke the lavish tongue when it doth utter	
	The breath of falsehood not charactered there.	
Warwick	Far be it from the honour of my age	
	That I should owe bright gold and render lead.	
	Age is a cynic, not a flatterer.	310
	I say again, that I if knew your grief,	
	And that by me it may be lessenèd,	
	My proper harm should buy your highness' good.	
King	These are the vulgar tenders of false men,	
	That never pay the duty of their words.	315

Thou wilt not stick to swear what thou hast said,
But when thou know'st my grief's condition,
This rash disgorgèd vomit of thy word
Thou wilt eat up again and leave me helpless.

Warwick By heaven I will not, though your majesty   320
Did bid me run upon your sword and die.

King Say that my grief is no way medicinable,
But by the loss and bruising of thine honour.

Warwick If nothing but that loss may vantage you,
I would account that loss my vantage too.   325

King Think'st that thou canst unswear thy oath again?

Warwick I cannot, nor I would not if I could.

King But if thou dost, what shall I say to thee?

Warwick What may be said to any perjured villain,
That breaks the sacred warrant of an oath.   330

King What wilt thou say to one that breaks an oath?

Warwick That he hath broke his faith with God and man
And from them both stands excommunicate.

King What office were it to suggest a man
To break a lawful and religious vow?   335

Warwick An office for the devil, not for man.

King That devil's office must thou do for me,
Or break thy oath, and cancel all the bonds
Of love and duty 'twixt thyself and me.
And therefore Warwick, if thou art thyself,   340
The lord and master of thy word and oath,
Go to thy daughter and in my behalf
Command her, woo her, win her any ways,
To be my mistress and my secret love.
I will not stand to hear thee make reply,   345
Thy oath break hers or let thy sovereign die.   *Exit*

Warwick   O doting King, O detestable office!
             Well may I tempt myself to wrong myself,
             When he hath sworn me by the name of God
             To break a vow made by the name of God.   350
             What if I swear by this right hand of mine,
             To cut this right hand off? The better way
             Were to profane the idol than confound it,
             But neither will I do, I'll keep mine oath,
             And to my daughter make a recantation   355
             Of all the virtue I have preached to her.
             I'll say she must forget her husband Salisbury,
             If she remember to embrace the King;
             I'll say an oath may easily be broken,
             But not so easily pardoned being broken;   360
             I'll say it is true charity to love,
             But not true love to be so charitable;
             I'll say his greatness may bear out the shame,
             But not his kingdom can buy out the sin;
             I'll say it is my duty to persuade,   365
             But not her honesty to give consent.

                        Enter the Countess

             See where she comes; was never father had
             Against his child an embassage so bad.

Countess   My lord and father, I have sought for you.
             My mother and the peers importune you   370
             To keep in promise of his majesty,
             And do your best to make his highness merry.

Warwick   How shall I enter in this graceless errand?
             I must not call her child, for where's the father,
             That will in such a suit seduce his child?   375
             Then 'wife of Salisbury' shall I so begin?
             No, he's my friend, and where is found the friend
             That will do friendship such endamagement? –
             Neither my daughter, nor my dear friend's wife,

I am not Warwick as thou think'st I am,   380
But an attorney from the court of hell
That thus have housed my spirit in his form,
To do a message to thee from the King.
The mighty King of England dotes on thee:
He that hath power to take away thy life   385
Hath power to take thy honour; then consent
To pawn thine honour rather than thy life.
Honour is often lost and got again,
But life once gone hath no recovery.
The sun that withers hay doth nourish grass;   390
The King that would distain thee, will advance thee.
The poets write that great Achilles' spear
Could heal the wound it made: the moral is,
What mighty men misdo, they can amend.
The lion doth become his bloody jaws,   395
And grace his foragement by being mild
When vassal fear lies trembling at his feet.
The King will in his glory hide thy shame,
And those that gaze on him to find out thee
Will lose their eyesight looking in the sun.   400
What can one drop of poison harm the sea,
Whose hugy vastures can digest the ill,
And make it lose his operation?
The king's great name will temper thy misdeeds,
And give the bitter potion of reproach   405
A sugared, sweet, and most delicious taste.
Besides it is no harm to do the thing
Which without shame could not be left undone.
Thus have I in his majesty's behalf
Apparelled sin in virtuous sentences,   410
And dwell upon thy answer in his suit.

Countess   Unnatural besiege, woe me unhappy,
To have escaped the danger of my foes,
And to be ten times worse envired by friends.

Hath he no means to stain my honest blood,   415
But to corrupt the author of my blood
To be his scandalous and vile solicitor?
No marvel though the branches be then infected,
When poison hath encompassèd the root;
No marvel though the lep'rous infant die,   420
When the stern dame envenometh the dug.
Why then give sin a passport to offend,
And youth the dangerous reign of liberty;
Blot out the strict forbidding of the law,
And cancel every canon that prescribes   425
A shame for shame, or penance for offence.
No, let me die, if his too boist'rous will
Will have it so, before I will consent
To be an actor in his graceless lust.

Warwick   Why now thou speak'st as I would have thee speak,   430
And mark how I unsay my words again.
An honourable grave is more esteemed,
Than the polluted closet of a king;
The greater man, the greater is the thing,
Be it good or bad, that he shall undertake;   435
An unreputed mote, flying in the sun,
Presents a greater substance than it is;
The freshest summer's day doth soonest taint
The loathèd carrion that it seems to kiss;
Deep are the blows made with a mighty axe;   440
That sin doth ten times aggravate itself
That is committed in a holy place;
An evil deed done by authority
Is sin and subornation; deck an ape
In tissue, and the beauty of the robe   445
Adds but the greater scorn unto the beast.
A spacious field of reasons could I urge
Between his glory, daughter, and thy shame:
That poison shows worst in a golden cup,

Dark night seems darker by the lightning flash,   450
Lilies that fester smell far worse then weeds,
And every glory that inclines to sin,
The shame is treble by the opposite.
So leave I with my blessing in thy bosom,
Which then convert to a most heavy curse   455
When thou convert'st from honour's golden name,
To the black faction of bed-blotting shame.

Countess   I'll follow thee, and when my mind turns so,
My body sink my soul in endless woe.

Exeunt

SCENE FOUR

*Enter at one door Derby from France, at another
door Audley with a drum*

Derby	Thrice noble Audley, well encountered here.
	How is it with our sovereign and his peers?
Audley	'Tis full a fortnight since I saw his highness,
	What time he sent me forth to muster men,
	Which I accordingly have done, and bring them hither, 5
	In fair array before his majesty.
	What news, my lord of Derby, from the Emperor?
Derby	As good as we desire: the Emperor
	Hath yielded to his highness friendly aid,
	And makes our king lieutenant-general 10
	In all his lands and large dominions;
	Then *via* for the spacious bounds of France.
Audley	What, doth his highness leap to hear these news?
Derby	I have not yet found time to open them.
	The King is in his closet malcontent, 15
	For what I know not, but he gave in charge,
	Till after dinner none should interrupt him.
	The Countess Salisbury and her father Warwick,
	Artois and all, look underneath the brows.
Audley	Undoubtedly then something is amiss. 20

Enter the King

Derby	The trumpets sound, the King is now abroad.
Audley	Here comes his highness.

Derby	Befall my sovereign all my sovereign's wish.
King	Ah that thou wert a witch to make it so.
Derby	The Emperor greeteth you. 24
King	Would it were the Countess.
Derby	And hath accorded to your highness' suit.
King	Thou liest, she hath not, but I would she had.
Audley	All love and duty to my lord the King.
King	Well all but one is none, what news with you?
Audley	I have, my liege, levied those horse and foot, 30
	According as your charge, and brought them hither.
King	Then let those foot trudge hence upon those horse,
	According to our discharge and be gone.
	Derby, I'll look upon the Countess' mind anon.
Derby	The Countess' mind, my liege? 35
King	I mean the Emperor, leave me alone.
Audley	What's in his mind?
Derby	Let's leave him to his humour.

Exeunt Audley and Derby

King	Thus from the heart's abundance speaks the tongue:
	Countess for Emperor, and indeed why not?
	She is as imperator over me, and I to her 40
	Am as a kneeling vassal that observes
	The pleasure or displeasure of her eye.

Enter Lodowick

What says the more than Cleopatra's match,
To Caesar now?

Lodowick	That yet, my liege, ere night,
	She will resolve your majesty. 45

King   What drum is this that thunders forth this march,
            To start the tender Cupid in my bosom?
            Poor sheepskin, how it brawls with him that beateth it.
            Go break the thund'ring parchment bottom out,
            And I will teach it to conduct sweet lines   50
            Unto the bosom of a heavenly nymph,
            For I will use it as my writing paper,
            And so reduce him from a scolding drum,
            To be the herald and dear counsel-bearer
            Betwixt a goddess and a mighty king.   55
            Go bid the drummer learn to touch the lute,
            Or hang him in the braces of his drum,
            For now we think it an uncivil thing
            To trouble heaven with such harsh resounds. Away!

                                                    Exit Lodowick

            The quarrel that I have requires no arms   60
            But these of mine, and these shall meet my foe
            In a deep march of penetrable groans;
            My eyes shall be my arrows, and my sighs
            Shall serve me as the vantage of the wind,
            To whirl away my sweetest artillery.   65
            Ah but alas, she wins the sun of me,
            For that is she herself, and thence it comes,
            That poets term the wanton warrior blind;
            But love hath eyes as judgement to his steps,
            Till too much lovèd glory dazzles them.   70
            How now?

                            Enter Lodowick

Lodowick   My liege, the drum that struck the lusty march
            Stands with Prince Edward, your thrice valiant son.   *Exit*

                          Enter Prince Edward

King   I see the boy, oh how his mother's face,
            Modelled in his, corrects my strayed desire,   75

And rates my heart, and chides my thievish eye,
Who being rich enough in seeing her,
Yet seeks elsewhere; and basest theft is that
Which cannot cloak itself on poverty.
Now boy, what news?   80

Prince   I have assembled, my dear lord and father,
The choicest buds of all our English blood
For our affairs to France, and here we come
To take direction from your majesty.

King   Still do I see in him delineate   85
His mother's visage, those his eyes are hers,
Who looking wistly on me, make me blush,
For faults against themselves give evidence.
Lust is a fire, and men like lanterns show
Light lust within themselves, even through themselves. 90
Away loose silks of wavering vanity!
Shall the large limit of fair Brittany
By me be overthrown, and shall I not
Master this little mansion of myself?
Give me an armour of eternal steel,   95
I go to conquer kings, and shall I not then
Subdue myself, and be my enemies' friend?
It must not be. Come boy, forward, advance,
Let's with our colours sweet the air of France.

                         Enter Lodowick

Lodowick My liege, the Countess with a smiling cheer   100
Desires access unto your majesty.

King   Why there it goes, that very smile of hers,
Hath ransomed captive France, and set the king,
The dauphin, and the peers at liberty. –   104
Go leave me Ned, and revel with thy friends.   *Exit Prince*

Thy mother is but black, and thou like her
Dost put it in my mind how foul she is.

Go fetch the Countess hither in thy hand,   *Exit Lodowick*
And let her chase away these winter clouds,
For she gives beauty both to heaven and earth.   110
The sin is more to hack and hew poor men,
Than to embrace in an unlawful bed
The register of all rarieties
Since leathern Adam till this youngest hour.

Enter the Countess and Lodowick

King   Go Lod'wick, put thy hand into thy purse,   115
              Play, spend, give, riot, waste, do what thou wilt,
              So thou wilt hence a while and leave me here.
                                                  Exit Lodowick

              Now my soul's playfellow, art thou come
              To speak the more than heavenly word of yea
              To my objection in thy beauteous love?   120

Countess   My father on his blessing hath commanded –

King   That thou shalt yield to me.

Countess   Ay dear my liege, your due.

King   And that, my dearest love, can be no less,
              Than right for right, and render love for love.

Countess   Than wrong for wrong, and endless hate for hate.   125
              But sith I see your majesty so bent,
              That my unwillingness, my husband's love,
              Your high estate, nor no respect respected,
              Can be my help, but that your mightiness
              Will overbear and awe these dear regards,   130
              I bind my discontent to my content,
              And what I would not, I'll compel I will,
              Provided that yourself remove those lets
              That stand between your highness' love and mine.

King   Name them, fair Countess, and by heaven I will.   135

Countess	It is their lives that stand between our love That I would have choked up, my sovereign.
King	Whose lives, my lady?
Countess	My thrice loving liege, Your Queen, and Salisbury my wedded husband, Who living have that title in our love 140 That we cannot bestow but by their death.
King	Thy opposition is beyond our law.
Countess	So is your desire. If the law Can hinder you to execute the one, Let it forbid you to attempt the other. 145 I cannot think you love me as you say, Unless you do make good what you have sworn.
King	No more, thy husband and the Queen shall die. Fairer thou art by far than Hero was, Beardless Leander not so strong as I: 150 He swam an easy current for his love, But I will through a Hellespont of blood, To arrive at Sestos where my Hero lies.
Countess	Nay, you'll do more, you'll make the river too With their heart bloods that keep our love asunder, 155 Of which my husband and your wife are twain.
King	Thy beauty makes them guilty of their death, And gives in evidence that they shall die, Upon which verdict I their judge condemn them.
Countess	O perjured beauty, more corrupted judge! 160 When to the great star-chamber o'er our heads The universal sessions calls to count This packing evil, we both shall tremble for it.
King	What says my fair love, is she resolute?

Countess	Resolved to be dissolved, and therefore this:	165

Keep but thy word, great King, and I am thine.
Stand where thou dost, I'll part a little from thee
And see how I will yield me to thy hands:
Here by my side doth hang my wedding knives;
Take thou the one, and with it kill thy queen,   170
And learn by me to find her where she lies,
And with this other, I'll dispatch my love,
Which now lies fast asleep within my heart.
When they are gone, then I'll consent to love.
Stir not, lascivious King, to hinder me;   175
My resolution is more nimbler far
Than thy prevention can be in my rescue.
An if thou stir, I strike; therefore stand still,
And hear the choice that I will put thee to:
Either swear to leave thy most unholy suit,   180
And never henceforth to solicit me,
Or else by heaven, this sharp pointed knife
Shall stain thy earth with that which thou wouldst stain,
My poor chaste blood. Swear Edward, swear,
Or I will strike and die before thee here.   185

King   Even by that power I swear that gives me now
The power to be ashamèd of myself,
I never mean to part my lips again
In any words that tends to such a suit.
Arise true English lady, whom our isle   190
May better boast of than ever Roman might
Of her whose ransacked treasury hath tasked
The vain endeavour of so many pens.
Arise, and be my fault thy honour's fame,
Which after ages shall enrich thee with.   195
I am awakèd from this idle dream.
Warwick, my son, Derby, Artois, and Audley,
Brave warriors all, where are you all this while?

Enter all

Warwick, I make thee Warden of the North,
Thou Prince of Wales, and Audley, straight to sea,   200
Scour to Newhaven, some there stay for me.
Myself, Artois, and Derby will through Flanders,
To greet our friends there, and to crave their aid,
This night will scarce suffice me to discover
My folly's siege against a faithful lover,   205
For ere the sun shall gild the eastern sky
We'll wake him with our martial harmony.

Exeunt

SCENE FIVE

Enter King John of France, his two sons,
Charles of Normandy and Philip, and the Duke of Lorraine

King John   Here till our navy of a thousand sail
Have made a breakfast to our foe by sea,
Let us encamp to wait their happy speed.
Lorraine, what readiness is Edward in?
How hast thou heard that he provided is   5
Of martial furniture for this exploit?

Lorraine   To lay aside unnecessary soothing,
And not to spend the time in circumstance,
'Tis bruited for a certainty my lord,
That he's exceeding strongly fortified;   10
His subjects flock as willingly to war
As if unto a triumph they were led.

Charles   England was wont to harbour malcontents,
Bloodthirsty and seditious Catilines,
Spendthrifts, and such as gape for nothing else   15
But change and alteration of the state,
And is it possible
That they are now so loyal in themselves?

Lorraine   All but the Scot, who solemnly protests,
As heretofore I have informed his grace,   20
Never to sheathe his sword or take a truce.

King John   Ah, that's the anch'rage of some better hope.
But on the other side, to think what friends
King Edward hath retained in Netherland,
Among those ever-bibbing epicures,   25
Those frothy Dutchmen puffed with double beer,

That drink and swill in every place they come,
Doth not a little aggravate mine ire.
Besides we hear the Emperor conjoins,
And stalls him in his own authority.   30
But all the mightier that their number is,
The greater glory reaps the victory.
Some friends have we besides domestic power,
The stern Polonian and the warlike Dane,
The king of Bohemia and of Sicily,   35
Are all become confederates with us,
And as I think are marching hither apace.
But soft, I hear the music of their drums,
By which I guess that their approach is near.

Enter the King of Bohemia with Danes,
and a Polonian Captain with other soldiers another way

Bohemia   King John of France, as league and neighbourhood   40
           Requires when friends are any way distressed,
           I come to aid thee with my country's force.

Captain   And from great Moscow, fearful to the Turk,
           And lofty Poland, nurse of hardy men,
           I bring these servitors to fight for thee,   45
           Who willingly will venture in thy cause.

King John Welcome Bohemian king, and welcome all,
           This your great kindness I will not forget.
           Besides your plentiful rewards in crowns
           That from our treasury ye shall receive,   50
           There comes a hare-brained nation decked in pride,
           The spoil of whom will be a treble gain.
           And now my hope is full, my joy complete:
           At sea we are as puissant as the force
           Of Agamemnon in the haven of Troy;   55
           By land with Xerxes we compare of strength,
           Whose soldiers drank up rivers in their thirst.
           Then Bayard-like, blind overweening Ned,

To reach at our imperial diadem,
Is either to be swallowed of the waves,   60
Or hacked a-pieces when thou com'st ashore.

Enter Mariner

Mariner   Near to the coast I have descried, my lord,
As I was busy in my watchful charge,
The proud armada of king Edward's ships,
Which at the first far off when I did ken,   65
Seemed as it were a grove of withered pines,
But drawing near, their glorious bright aspect,
Their streaming ensigns wrought of coloured silk,
Like to a meadow full of sundry flowers
Adorns the naked bosom of the earth.   70
Majestical the order of their course,
Figuring the hornèd circle of the moon,
And on the top gallant of the admiral,
And likewise all the handmaids of his train,
The arms of England and of France unite   75
Are quartered equally by herald's art;
Thus tightly carried with a merry gale,
They plough the ocean hitherward amain.

King John   Dare he already crop the fleur-de-lis?
I hope the honey being gathered thence,   80
He with the spider afterward approached
Shall suck forth deadly venom from the leaves.
But where's our navy, how are they prepared
To wing themselves against this flight of ravens?

Mariner   They having knowledge brought them by the scouts,   85
Did break from anchor straight, and puffed with rage,
No otherwise than were their sails with wind,
Made forth as when the empty eagle flies
To satisfy his hungry griping maw.

King John   There's for thy news, return unto thy barque,   90
And if thou scape the bloody stroke of war

And do survive the conflict, come again,
And let us hear the manner of the fight.   *Exit Mariner*
Mean space my lords, 'tis best we be dispersed,
To several places lest they chance to land.   95
First you my lord, with your Bohemian troops,
Shall pitch your battles on the lower hand;
My eldest son, the Duke of Normandy,
Together with this aid of Muscovites,
Shall climb the higher ground another way;   100
Here in the middle coast betwixt you both,
Philip my youngest boy and I will lodge.
So lords be gone, and look unto your charge,
You stand for France, an empire fair and large.

Exeunt all but King John and Philip

Now tell me Philip, what is thy conceit,   105
Touching the challenge that the English make?

Philip   I say my lord, claim Edward what he can,
And bring he ne'er so plain a pedigree,
'Tis you are in possession of the crown,
And that's the surest point of all the law.   110
But were it not, yet ere he should prevail,
I'll make a conduit of my dearest blood,
Or chase those straggling upstarts home again.

King John Well said young Philip, call for bread and wine,
That we may cheer our stomachs with repast,   115
To look our foes more sternly in the face.

The battle heard afar off

Now is begun the heavy day at sea.
Fight Frenchmen, fight, be like the field of bears,
When they defend their younglings in their caves.
Steer, angry Nemesis, the happy helm,   120
That with the sulphur battles of your rage,
The English fleet may be dispersed and sunk.

Shot

Philip	O father, how this echoing cannon shot	
	Like sweet harmony digests my cates.	

King John   Now boy, thou hear'st what thund'ring terror 'tis   125
To buckle for a kingdom's sovereignty.
The earth with giddy trembling when it shakes,
Or when the exhalations of the air
Breaks in extremity of lightning flash,
Affrights not more than kings when they dispose   130
To show the rancour of their high-swoll'n hearts.

Retreat

Retreat is sounded, one side hath the worse.
O if it be the French, sweet fortune turn,
And in thy turning change the forward winds,
That with advantage of a favouring sky,   135
Our men may vanquish and th'other fly.

Enter Mariner

My heart misgives, say mirror of pale death,
To whom belongs the honour of this day.
Relate I pray thee, if thy breath will serve,
The sad discourse of this discomfiture.   140

Mariner   I will my lord.
My gracious sovereign, France hath ta'en the foil,
And boasting Edward triumphs with success.
These iron-hearted navies,
When last I was reporter to your grace,   145
Both full of angry spleen, of hope and fear,
Hasting to meet each other in the face,
At last conjoined, and by their admiral,
Our admiral encountered many shot.
By this, the other, that beheld these twain   150
Give earnest penny of a further wrack,

Like fiery dragons took their haughty flight,
And likewise meeting, from their smoky wombs,
Sent many grim ambassadors of death.
Then 'gan the day to turn to gloomy night,   155
And darkness did as well enclose the quick
As those that were but newly reft of life.
No leisure served for friends to bid farewell,
And if it had, the hideous noise was such
As each to other seemèd deaf and dumb.   160
Purple the sea, whose channel filled as fast
With streaming gore that from the maimèd fell,
As did her gushing moisture break into
The crannied cleftures of the through-shot planks.
Here flew a head dissevered from the trunk,   165
There mangled arms and legs were tossed aloft
As when a whirlwind takes the summer dust,
And scatters it in middle of the air.
Then might ye see the reeling vessels split,
And tottering sink into the ruthless flood,   170
Until their lofty tops were seen no more.
All shifts were tried both for defence and hurt,
And now the effect of valour and of force,
Of resolution and of cowardice
Were lively pictured, how the one for fame,   175
The other by compulsion laid about;
Much did the Nonpareille, that brave ship,
So did the black snake of Boulogne, than which
A bonnier vessel never yet spread sail;
But all in vain, both sun, the wind and tide,   180
Revolted all unto our foemen's side,
That we perforce were fain to give them way,
And they are landed. Thus my tale is done,
We have untimely lost, and they have won.

King John   Then rests there nothing but with present speed,   185
To join our several forces all in one,

And bid them battle ere they range too far.
Come gentle Philip, let us hence depart,
This soldier's words have pierced thy father's heart.

Exeunt

SCENE SIX

Enter two Frenchmen. A woman and two little children
meet them, and other citizens

1 Frenchman Well met my masters: how now, what's the news,
And wherefore are ye laden thus with stuff?
What, is it quarter day that you remove,
And carry bag and baggage too?

1 Citizen Quarter day, ay, and quartering day I fear: 5
Have ye not heard the news that flies abroad?

1 Frenchman What news?

2 Citizen How the French navy is destroyed at sea,
And that the English army is arrived.

1 Frenchman What then?   10

1 Citizen What then, quoth you? Why, is't not time to fly,
When envy and destruction is so nigh?

1 Frenchman Content thee man, they are far enough from hence,
And will be met, I warrant ye, to their cost,
Before they break so far into the realm.   15

1 Citizen Ay, so the grasshopper doth spend the time
In mirthful jollity till winter come,
And then too late he would redeem his time,
When frozen cold hath nipped his careless head.
He that no sooner will provide a cloak   20
Than when he sees it doth begin to rain,
May peradventure for his negligence
Be throughly washed when he suspects it not.
We that have charge, and such a train as this,

Must look in time, to look for them and us,   25
Lest when we would, we cannot be relieved.

1 Frenchman Belike you then despair of ill success,
And think your country will be subjugate.

2 Citizen We cannot tell, 'tis good to fear the worst.

1 Frenchman Yet rather fight than like unnatural sons,   30
Forsake your loving parents in distress.

1 Citizen Tush, they that have already taken arms
Are many fearful millions in respect
Of that small handful of our enemies;
But 'tis a rightful quarrel must prevail.   35
Edward is son unto our late king's sister,
Where John Valois is three degrees removed.

Woman   Besides, there goes a prophesy abroad,
Published by one that was a friar once,
Whose oracles have many times proved true;   40
And now he says the time will shortly come,
Whenas a lion rousèd in the west
Shall carry hence the fleur-de-lis of France.
These I can tell ye and suchlike surmises
Strike many Frenchmen cold unto the heart.   45

Enter a Frenchman

3 Frenchman Fly countrymen and citizens of France.
Sweet flow'ring peace, the root of happy life,
Is quite abandoned and expulsed the land,
Instead of whom ransack-constraining war
Sits like to ravens upon your houses' tops,   50
Slaughter and mischief walk within your streets
And unrestrained make havoc as they pass,
The form whereof even now myself beheld,
Upon this fair mountain whence I came.
For so far off as I directed mine eyes,   55

I might perceive five cities all on fire,
Cornfields and vineyards burning like an oven,
And as the leaking vapour in the wind
Turned but aside, I likewise might discern
The poor inhabitants, escaped the flame, 60
Fall numberless upon the soldiers' pikes.
Three ways these dreadful ministers of wrath
Do tread the measures of their tragic march:
Upon the right hand comes the conquering King,
Upon the left his hot unbridled son, 65
And in the midst their nation's glittering host,
All which though distant yet conspire in one,
To leave a desolation where they come.
Fly therefore citizens, if you be wise,
Seek out some habitation further off. 70
Here if you stay your wives will be abused,
Your treasure shared before your weeping eyes;
Shelter yourselves for now the storm doth rise.
Away, away, methinks I hear their drums.
Ah wretched France, I greatly fear thy fall; 75
Thy glory shaketh like a tottering wall.

Exeunt

SCENE SEVEN

Enter King Edward and the Earl of Derby with soldiers,
and Gobin de Grace

King   Where's the Frenchman by whose cunning guide
We found the shallow of this River Somme,
And had direction how to pass the sea?

Gobin   Here my good lord.

King   How art thou called? Tell me thy name.   5

Gobin   Gobin de Grace, if please your excellence.

King   Then Gobin, for the service thou hast done,
We here enlarge and give thee liberty,
And for recompense beside this good,
Thou shalt receive five hundred marks in gold.   10
I know not how we should have met our son,
Whom now in heart I wish I might behold.

Enter Artois

Good news, my lord, the Prince is hard at hand,
And with him comes Lord Audley and the rest,
Whom since our landing we could never meet.   15

Enter Prince Edward, Lord Audley, and soldiers

King   Welcome fair Prince, how hast thou sped, my son,
Since thy arrival on the coast of France?

Prince   Successfully, I thank the gracious heavens.
Some of their strongest cities we have won,
As Harfleur, Lô, Crotoy, and Carentan,   20
And others wasted, leaving at our heels

A wide apparent field and beaten path,
For solitariness to progress in.
Yet those that would submit we kindly pardoned,
But who in scorn refused our proffered peace,   25
Endured the penalty of sharp revenge.

King   Ah France, why shouldst thou be thus obstinate,
          Against the kind embracement of thy friends?
          How gently had we thought to touch thy breast,
          And set our foot upon thy tender mould,   30
          But that in froward and disdainful pride
          Thou like a skittish and untamèd colt,
          Dost start aside and strike us with thy heels.
          But tell me Ned, in all thy warlike course,
          Hast thou not seen the usurping King of France?   35

Prince   Yes my good lord, and not two hours ago,
          With full a hundred thousand fighting men,
          Upon the one side of the river's bank
          And on the other, both his multitudes.
          I feared he would have cropped our smaller power, 40
          But happily perceiving your approach,
          He hath withdrawn himself to Crécy plains,
          Where as it seemeth by his good array
          He means to bid us battle presently.

King   He shall be welcome, that's the thing we crave.   45

          Enter King John, the Dukes of Normandy and Lorraine,
          the King of Bohemia, young Philip, and soldiers

King John Edward, know that John the true king of France,
          Musing thou shouldst encroach upon his land,
          And in thy tyrannous proceeding slay
          His faithful subjects and subvert his towns,
          Spits in thy face, and in this manner following,   50
          Upbraids thee with thine arrogant intrusion:
          First I condemn thee for a fugitive,

A thievish pirate, and a needy mate,
One that hath either no abiding place,
Or else inhabiting some barren soil,   55
Where neither herb or fruitful grain is had,
Dost altogether live by pilfering;
Next, insomuch thou hast infringed thy faith,
Broke league and solemn covenant made with me,
I hold thee for a false pernicious wretch;   60
And last of all, although I scorn to cope
With one so much inferior to myself,
Yet in respect thy thirst is all for gold,
Thy labour rather to be feared than loved,
To satisfy thy lust in either part   65
Here am I come and with me have I brought
Exceeding store of treasure, pearl, and coin.
Leave therefore now to persecute the weak,
And armèd ent'ring conflict with the armed,
Let it be seen 'mongst other petty thefts,   70
How thou canst win this pillage manfully.

King   If gall or wormwood have a pleasant taste,
Then is thy salutation honey-sweet,
But as the one hath no such property,
So is the other most satirical.   75
Yet wot how I regard thy worthless taunts:
If thou have uttered them to foil my fame,
Or dim the reputation of my birth,
Know that thy wolfish barking cannot hurt;
If slyly to insinuate with the world,   80
And with a strumpet's artificial line,
To paint thy vicious and deformèd cause,
Be well assured the counterfeit will fade,
And in the end thy foul defects be seen.
But if thou didst it to provoke me on,   85
As who should say I were but timorous,
Or coldly negligent did need a spur,

Bethink thyself how slack I was at sea,
How since my landing I have won no towns,
Entered no further but upon thy coast, 90
And there have ever since securely slept;
But if I have been otherwise employed,
Imagine, Valois, whether I intend
To skirmish not for pillage but for the crown
Which thou dost wear and that I vow to have, 95
Or one of us shall fall into his grave.

Prince   Look not for cross invectives at our hands,
Or railing execrations of despite.
Let creeping serpents hide in hollow banks,
Sting with their tongues; we have remorseless swords, 100
And they shall plead for us and our affairs.
Yet thus much briefly, by my father's leave:
As all the immodest poison of thy throat
Is scandalous and most notorious lies,
And our pretended quarrel is truly just, 105
So end the battle when we meet today:
May either of us prosper and prevail,
Or luckless cursed, receive eternal shame.

King   That needs no further question, and I know
His conscience witnesseth it is my right. 110
Therefore Valois, say wilt thou yet resign,
Before the sickle's thrust into the corn,
Or that enkindled fury turn to flame?

King John   Edward, I know what right thou hast in France,
And ere I basely will resign my crown, 115
This champaign field shall be a pool of blood,
And all our prospect as a slaughterhouse.

Prince   Ay that approves thee, tyrant, what thou art,
No father, king, or shepherd of thy realm,
But one that tears her entrails with thy hands, 120
And like a thirsty tiger suck'st her blood.

Audley	You peers of France, why do you follow him,
	That is so prodigal to spend your lives?
Charles	Whom should they follow, agèd impotent,
	But he that is their true-born sovereign? 125
King	Upbraid'st thou him because within his face
	Time hath engraved deep characters of age?
	Know these grave scholars of experience
	Like stiff-grown oaks will stand immovable
	When whirlwind quickly turns up younger trees. 130
Derby	Was ever any of thy father's house
	King, but thyself, before this present time?
	Edward's great lineage by the mother's side
	Five hundred years hath held the sceptre up.
	Judge then, conspirators, by this descent, 135
	Which is the true-born sovereign, this or that.
Philip	Father, range your battles, prate no more,
	These English fain would spend the time in words,
	That night approaching, they might escape unfought.
King John	Lords and my loving subjects, now's the time, 140
	That your intended force must bide the touch.
	Therefore my friends, consider this in brief:
	He that you fight for is your natural king,
	He against whom you fight a foreigner;
	He that you fight for rules in clemency, 145
	And reigns you with a mild and gentle bit,
	He against whom you fight, if he prevail,
	Will straight enthrone himself in tyranny,
	Make slaves of you, and with a heavy hand
	Curtail and curb your sweetest liberty. 150
	Then to protect your country and your king,
	Let but the haughty courage of your hearts
	Answer the number of your able hands,
	And we shall quickly chase these fugitives.
	For what's this Edward but a belly-god, 155

A tender and lascivious wantonness,
That th'other day was almost dead for love,
And what I pray you is his goodly guard?
Such as but scant them of their chines of beef,
And take away their downy feather beds,   160
And presently they are as resty-stiff,
As 'twere a many over-ridden jades.
Then Frenchmen, scorn that such should be your lords
And rather bind ye them in captive bonds.

All French   *Vive le roi*, God save King John of France.   165

King John   Now on this plain of Crécy spread yourselves,
And Edward, when thou dar'st, begin the fight.

               Exeunt King John, Bohemia, and French

King   We presently will meet thee, John of France;
And English lords, let us resolve the day,
Either to clear us of that scandalous crime,   170
Or be entombèd in our innocence.
And Ned, because this battle is the first
That ever yet thou fought'st in pitchèd field,
As ancient custom is of martialists,
To dub thee with the type of chivalry,   175
In solemn manner we will give thee arms.
Come therefore heralds, orderly bring forth
A strong attirement for the Prince my son.

     Enter four heralds bringing in a coat armour,
        a helmet, a lance, and a shield

Edward Plantagenet, in the name of God,
As with this armour I impale thy breast,   180
So be thy noble unrelenting heart
Walled in with flint of matchless fortitude,
That never base affections enter there.
Fight and be valiant, conquer where thou com'st.
Now follow lords, and do him honour too.   185

Derby	Edward Plantagenet, Prince of Wales,
	As I do set this helmet on thy head,
	Wherewith the chamber of thy brain is fenced,
	So may thy temples with Bellona's hand
	Be still adorned with laurel victory. 190
	Fight and be valiant, conquer where thou com'st.

Audley	Edward Plantagenet, Prince of Wales,
	Receive this lance into thy manly hand,
	Use it in fashion of a brazen pen,
	To draw forth bloody stratagems in France 195
	And print thy valiant deeds in honour's book.
	Fight and be valiant, conquer where thou com'st.

Artois	Edward Plantagenet, Prince of Wales,
	Hold take this target, wear it on thy arm,
	And may the view thereof, like Perseus' shield, 200
	Astonish and transform thy gazing foes
	To senseless images of meagre death.
	Fight and be valiant, conquer where thou com'st.

King	Now wants there naught but knighthood, which deferred
	We leave till thou hast won it in the field. 205

Prince	My gracious father and ye forward peers,
	This honour you have done me animates
	And cheers my green yet scarce-appearing strength
	With comfortable good-presaging signs,
	No otherwise than did old Jacob's words, 210
	Whenas he breathed his blessings on his sons.
	These hallowed gifts of yours when I profane,
	Or use them not to glory of my God,
	To patronage the fatherless and poor,
	Or for the benefit of England's peace, 215
	Be numb my joints, wax feeble both mine arms,
	Wither my heart, that like a sapless tree,
	I may remain the map of infamy.

King   Then thus our steelèd battles shall be ranged,
         The leading of the vaward, Ned, is thine,   220
         To dignify whose lusty spirit the more
         We temper it with Audley's gravity,
         That courage and experience joined in one,
         Your manage may be second unto none.
         For the main battles I will guide myself,   225
         And Derby in the rearward march behind,
         That orderly disposed and set in 'ray,
         Let us to horse and God grant us the day.

                                                        Exeunt

SCENE EIGHT

Alarum. Enter a many Frenchmen flying.
After them Prince Edward running.
Then enter King John and the Duke of Lorraine

King John   O Lorraine say, what mean our men to fly?
            Our number is far greater than our foe's.

Lorraine   The garrison of Genoese, my lord,
            That came from Paris, weary with their march,
            Grudging to be so suddenly employed,   5
            No sooner in the forefront took their place
            But straight retiring so dismayed the rest
            As likewise they betook themselves to flight,
            In which for haste to make a safe escape,
            More in the clustering throng are pressed to death   10
            Than by the enemy a thousandfold.

King John   O hapless fortune, let us yet assay,
            If we can counsel some of them to stay.

                                                        Exeunt

                Enter King Edward and Audley

King   Lord Audley, whiles our son is in the chase,
            Withdraw our powers unto this little hill,   15
            And here a season let us breathe ourselves.

Audley   I will, my lord.   *Exit*

                    Sound retreat

King   Just-dooming heaven, whose secret providence
            To our gross judgement is inscrutable,
            How are we bound to praise thy wondrous works,   20

That hast this day given way unto the right,
And made the wicked stumble at themselves.

Enter Artois

Artois   Rescue King Edward, rescue for thy son.

King   Rescue Artois? What, is he prisoner,
Or by violence fell beside his horse?   25

Artois   Neither my lord, but narrowly beset
With turning Frenchmen, whom he did pursue,
As 'tis impossible that he should scape,
Except your highness presently descend.

King   Tut, let him fight, we gave him arms today,   30
And he is labouring for a knighthood, man.

Enter Derby

Derby   The Prince my lord, the Prince, oh succour him,
He's close encompassed with a world of odds.

King   Then will he win a world of honour too,
If he by valour can redeem him thence.   35
If not, what remedy? We have more sons
Than one to comfort our declining age.

Enter Audley

Audley   Renownèd Edward, give me leave I pray,
To lead my soldiers where I may relieve
Your grace's son, in danger to be slain.   40
The snares of French, like emmets on a bank,
Muster about him whilst he lion-like,
Entangled in the net of their assaults,
Franticly rends and bites the woven toil,
But all in vain, he cannot free himself.   45

King   Audley content, I will not have a man,
On pain of death, sent forth to succour him:

This is the day ordained by destiny
To season his courage with those grievous thoughts,
That if he break out, Nestor's years on earth   50
Will make him savour still of this exploit.

Derby   Ah but he shall not live to see those days.

King   Why then his epitaph is lasting praise.

Audley   Yet good my lord, 'tis too much wilfulness
To let his blood be spilt that may be saved.   55

King   Exclaim no more, for none of you can tell
Whether a borrowed aid will serve or no.
Perhaps he is already slain or ta'en:
And dare a falcon when she's in her flight,
And ever after she'll be haggard-like.   60
Let Edward be delivered by our hands,
And still in danger he'll expect the like;
But if himself, himself redeem from thence,
He will have vanquished, cheerful, death and fear,
And ever after dread their force no more   65
Than if they were but babes or captive slaves.

Audley   O cruel father, farewell Edward then.

Derby   Farewell sweet Prince, the hope of chivalry.

Artois   O would my life might ransom him from death.

King   But soft, methinks I hear   70
The dismal charge of trumpets' loud retreat.
All are not slain I hope that went with him;
Some will return with tidings good or bad.

Enter Prince Edward in triumph, bearing in his hand
his shivered lance, and the King of Bohemia borne before,
wrapped in the colours. They run and embrace him

Audley   O joyful sight, victorious Edward lives.

Derby	Welcome brave Prince.
King	Welcome Plantagenet. 75

The Prince kneels and kisses his father's hand

Prince   First having done my duty as beseemed,
Lords, I regreet you all with hearty thanks.
And now behold, after my winter's toil,
My painful voyage on the boist'rous sea
Of war's devouring gulfs and steely rocks,   80
I bring my freight unto the wishèd port,
My summer's hope, my travail's sweet reward,
And here with humble duty I present
This sacrifice, this first fruit of my sword,
Cropped and cut down even at the gate of death: 85
The King of Boheme, father, whom I slew,
Whose thousands had entrenched me round about,
And lay as thick upon my battered crest,
As on an anvil with their ponderous glaives.
Yet marble courage still did underprop,   90
And when my weary arms with often blows,
Like the continual labouring woodman's axe
That is enjoined to fell a load of oaks,
Began to falter, straight I would recover
My gifts you gave me, and my zealous vow,   95
And then new courage made me fresh again,
That in despite I carved my passage forth,
And put the multitude to speedy flight.
Lo thus hath Edward's hand filled your request,
And done I hope the duty of a knight.   100

His sword is borne by a soldier

King   Ay, well thou hast deserved a knighthood, Ned,
And therefore with thy sword, yet reeking warm
With blood of those that fought to be thy bane,
Arise Prince Edward, trusty knight at arms.

This day thou hast confounded me with joy,   105
And proved thyself fit heir unto a king.

Prince   Here is a note, my gracious lord, of those
That in this conflict of our foes were slain:
Eleven princes of esteem, four score barons,
A hundred and twenty knights, and thirty thousand   110
Common soldiers, and of our men a thousand.

[King]   Our God be praised. Now John of France, I hope
Thou know'st King Edward for no wantonness,
No lovesick cockney, nor his soldiers jades.
But which way is the fearful king escaped?   115

Prince   Towards Poitiers, noble father, and his sons.

King   Ned, thou and Audley shall pursue them still.
Myself and Derby will to Calais straight,
And there begirt that haven town with siege.
Now lies it on an upshot, therefore strike,   120
And wistly follow whiles the game's on foot.
What picture's this?

Prince   A pelican, my lord,
Wounding her bosom with her crooked beak,
That so her nest of young ones might be fed
With drops of blood that issue from her heart,   125
The motto *Sic et vos*: 'and so should you'.

                                                    Exeunt

SCENE NINE

Enter Lord Montfort with a coronet in his hand,
with him the Earl of Salisbury

Montfort My lord of Salisbury, since by your aid
Mine enemy Sir Charles of Blois is slain,
And I again am quietly possessed
In Bretagne's dukedom, know that I resolve,
For this kind furtherance of your king and you, 5
To swear allegiance to his majesty:
In sign whereof receive this coronet.
Bear it unto him, and withal mine oath,
Never to be but Edward's faithful friend.

Salisbury I take it Montfort, thus I hope ere long 10
The whole dominions of the realm of France
Will be surrendered to his conquering hand.

Exit Montfort

Now if I knew but safely how to pass,
I would at Calais gladly meet his grace,
Whither I am by letters certified 15
That he intends to have his host removed.
It shall be so, this policy will serve.
Ho, who's within? Bring Villiers to me.

Enter Villiers

Villiers, thou know'st thou art my prisoner,
And that I might for ransom, if I would, 20
Require of thee a hundred thousand francs,
Or else retain and keep thee captive still;
But so it is, that for a smaller charge

Thou mayst be quit, an if thou wilt thyself.
And this it is, procure me but a passport   25
Of Charles the Duke of Normandy, that I
Without restraint may have recourse to Calais
Through all the countries where he hath to do,
Which thou mayst easily obtain I think,
By reason I have often heard thee say,   30
He and thou were students once together;
And then thou shalt be set at liberty.
How say'st thou, wilt thou undertake to do it?

Villiers   I will my lord, but I must speak with him.

Salisbury   Why so thou shalt, take horse and post from hence.   35
Only before thou goest, swear by thy faith
That if thou canst not compass my desire,
Thou wilt return my prisoner back again,
And that shall be sufficient warrant for me.

Villiers   To that condition I agree, my lord,   40
And will unfeignedly perform the same.   *Exit*

Salisbury   Farewell Villiers.
Thus once I mean to try a Frenchman's faith.   *Exit*

SCENE TEN

Enter King Edward and Derby with soldiers

King   Since they refuse our proffered league, my lord,
And will not ope their gates and let us in,
We will entrench ourselves on every side,
That neither victuals, nor supply of men
May come to succour this accursèd town.   5
Famine shall combat where our swords are stopped.

Enter six poor Frenchmen

Derby   The promised aid that made them stand aloof
Is now retired and gone another way:
It will repent them of their stubborn will.
But what are these poor ragged slaves, my lord?   10

King   Ask what they are, it seems they come from Calais.

Derby   You wretched patterns of despair and woe,
What are you, living men or gliding ghosts,
Crept from your graves to walk upon the earth?

1 Poor Frenchman
             No ghosts my lord, but men that breathe a life   15
Far worse than is the quiet sleep of death.
We are distressèd poor inhabitants
That long have been diseasèd, sick, and lame,
And now because we are not fit to serve,
The captain of the town hath thrust us forth,   20
That so expense of victuals may be saved.

King   A charitable deed no doubt, and worthy praise!
But how do you imagine then to speed?

We are your enemies; in such a case,
We can no less but put ye to the sword,   25
Since when we proffered truce, it was refused.

1 Poor Frenchman

An if your grace no otherwise vouchsafe,
As welcome death is unto us as life.

King

Poor silly men, much wronged, and more distressed.
Go Derby go, and see they be relieved,   30
Command that victuals be appointed them,
And give to every one five crowns apiece.

Exeunt Derby and Frenchmen

The lion scorns to touch the yielding prey,
And Edward's sword must flesh itself in such
As wilful stubbornness hath made perverse.   35

Enter Lord Percy

Lord Percy welcome, what's the news in England?

Percy

The Queen, my lord, commends her to your grace,
And from her highness, and the lord vicegerent,
I bring this happy tidings of success:
David of Scotland, lately up in arms,   40
Thinking belike he soonest should prevail,
Your highness being absent from the realm,
Is by the fruitful service of your peers,
And painful travail of the Queen herself,
That big with child was every day in arms,   45
Vanquished, subdued, and taken prisoner.

King

Thanks, Percy, for thy news with all my heart.
What was he took him prisoner in the field?

Percy

A squire my lord, John Copland is his name,
Who since entreated by her majesty,   50
Denies to make surrender of his prize

To any but unto your grace alone,
Whereat the Queen is grievously displeased.

King Well then we'll have a pursuivant dispatched
To summon Copland hither out of hand, 55
And with him he shall bring his prisoner king.

Percy The Queen's, my lord, herself by this at sea,
And purposeth as soon as wind will serve,
To land at Calais, and to visit you.

King She shall be welcome, and to wait her coming, 60
I'll pitch my tent near to the sandy shore.

Enter a Captain

Captain The burgesses of Calais, mighty king,
Have by a counsel willingly decreed
To yield the town and castle to your hands,
Upon condition it will please your grace 65
To grant them benefit of life and goods.

King They will so? Then belike they may command,
Dispose, elect, and govern as they list.
No sirrah, tell them since they did refuse
Our princely clemency at first proclaimed, 70
They shall not have it now although they would.
I will accept of naught but fire and sword,
Except within these two days six of them
That are the wealthiest merchants in the town
Come naked all but for their linen shirts, 75
With each a halter hanged about his neck,
And prostrate yield themselves upon their knees,
To be afflicted, hanged, or what I please.
And so you may inform their masterships.

Exeunt all but the Captain

Captain Why this it is to trust a broken staff. 80
Had we not been persuaded John our King

Would with his army have relieved the town,
We had not stood upon defiance so.
But now 'tis past that no man can recall,　　　　84
And better some do go to wrack than all.　　　　*Exit*

SCENE ELEVEN

Enter Charles of Normandy and Villiers

Charles	I wonder, Villiers, thou shouldst importune me
	For one that is our deadly enemy.

Villiers	Not for his sake, my gracious lord, so much	
	Am I become an earnest advocate,	
	As that thereby my ransom will be quit.	5

Charles	Thy ransom, man, why need'st thou talk of that?
	Art thou not free? And are not all occasions
	That happen for advantage of our foes
	To be accepted of and stood upon?

Villiers	No good my lord, except the same be just,	10
	For profit must with honour be commixed,	
	Or else our actions are but scandalous.	
	But letting pass these intricate objections,	
	Wilt please your highness to subscribe or no?	

Charles	Villiers I will not, nor I cannot do it;	15
	Salisbury shall not have his will so much	
	To claim a passport how it pleaseth himself.	

Villiers	Why then I know the extremity, my lord;
	I must return to prison whence I came.

Charles	Return I hope thou wilt not.	20
	What bird that hath escaped the fowler's gin,	
	Will not beware how she's ensnared again?	
	Or what is he so senseless and secure,	
	That having hardly passed a dangerous gulf,	
	Will put himself in peril there again?	25

Villiers	Ah but it is mine oath, my gracious lord,
	Which I in conscience may not violate,
	Or else a kingdom should not draw me hence.

Charles	Thine oath, why that doth bind thee to abide.	
	Hast thou not sworn obedience to thy prince?	30

Villiers	In all things that uprightly he commands;
	But either to persuade or threaten me
	Not to perform the covenant of my word
	Is lawless, and I need not to obey.

Charles	Why, is it lawful for a man to kill,	35
	And not to break a promise with his foe?	

Villiers	To kill, my lord, when war is once proclaimed,	
	So that our quarrel be for wrongs received,	
	No doubt is lawfully permitted us;	
	But in an oath we must be well advised	40
	How we do swear, and when we once have sworn,	
	Not to infringe it though we die therefor.	
	Therefore my lord, as willing I return	
	As if I were to fly to paradise.	

Charles	Stay my Villiers, thine honourable mind	45
	Deserves to be eternally admired.	
	Thy suit shall be no longer thus deferred:	
	Give me the paper, I'll subscribe to it,	
	And wheretofore I loved thee as Villiers,	
	Hereafter I'll embrace thee as myself.	50
	Stay and be still in favour with thy lord.	

Villiers	I humbly thank your grace, I must dispatch
	And send this passport first unto the earl,
	And then I will attend your highness' pleasure.

Charles	Do so Villiers, and Charles when he hath need,	55
	Be such his soldiers, howsoever he speed.	

Exit Villiers

Enter King John

King John Come Charles and arm thee, Edward is entrapped,
           The Prince of Wales is fall'n into our hands,
           And we have compassed him he cannot scape.

Charles   But will your highness fight today?   60

King John What else my son? He's scarce eight thousand strong,
           And we are threescore thousand at the least.

Charles   I have a prophecy, my gracious lord,
           Wherein is written what success is like
           To happen us in this outrageous war.   65
           It was delivered me at Crécy's field
           By one that is an aged hermit there:
           'When feathered fowl shall make thine army tremble,
           And flintstones rise and break the battle 'ray,
           Then think on him that doth not now dissemble   70
           For that shall be the hapless dreadful day.
           Yet in the end thy foot thou shalt advance
           As far in England, as thy foe in France.'

King John By this it seems we shall be fortunate:
           For as it is impossible that stones   75
           Should ever rise and break the battle 'ray,
           Or airy fowl make men in arms to quake,
           So is it like we shall not be subdued;
           Or say this might be true, yet in the end,
           Since he doth promise we shall drive him hence,   80
           And forage their country as they have done ours,
           By this revenge that loss will seem the less.
           But all are frivolous fancies, toys and dreams.
           Once we are sure we have ensnared the son,
           Catch we the father after how we can.   85

                                                          Exeunt

SCENE TWELVE

Enter Prince Edward, Audley, and others

Prince   Audley, the arms of death embrace us round,
And comfort have we none, save that to die
We pay sour earnest for a sweeter life.
At Crécy field our clouds of warlike smoke
Choked up those French mouths and dissevered them, 5
But now their multitudes of millions hide,
Masking as 'twere the beauteous burning sun,
Leaving no hope to us but sullen dark,
And eyeless terror of all-ending night.

Audley   This sudden, mighty, and expedient head 10
That they have made, fair prince, is wonderful.
Before us in the valley lies the king,
Vantaged with all that heaven and earth can yield,
His party stronger battled than our whole.
His son the braving Duke of Normandy, 15
Hath trimmed the mountain on our right hand up
In shining plate, that now the aspiring hill
Shows like a silver quarry, or an orb
Aloft the which the banners, bannerets,
And new-replenished pendants cuff the air 20
And beat the winds, that for their gaudiness,
Struggles to kiss them. On our left hand lies
Philip, the younger issue of the king,
Coting the other hill in such array,
That all his gilded upright pikes do seem 25
Straight trees of gold, the pendants leaves,
And their device of antique heraldry,
Quartered in colours seeming sundry fruits,

Makes it the orchard of the Hesperides.
Behind us two the hill doth bear his height, 30
For like a half-moon opening but one way,
It rounds us in. There at our backs are lodged
The fatal crossbows, and the battle there
Is governed by the rough Chatillion.
Then thus it stands: the valley for our flight 35
The king binds in, the hills on either hand
Are proudly royalizèd by his sons,
And on the hill behind stands certain death,
In pay and service with Chatillion.

Prince Death's name is much more mighty than his deeds. 40
Thy parcelling this power hath made it more
Than all the world, and call it but a power.
As many sands as these my hands can hold
Are but my handful of so many sands,
Easily ta'en up and quickly thrown away; 45
But if I stand to count them sand by sand
The number would confound my memory,
And make a thousand millions of a task,
Which briefly is no more indeed than one.
These quarters, squadrons, and these regiments, 50
Before, behind us, and on either hand,
Are but a power. When we name a man,
His hand, his foot, his head hath several strengths,
And being all but one self instant strength,
Why all this many, Audley, is but one, 55
And we can call it all but one man's strength.
He that hath far to go tells it by miles;
If he should tell the steps, it kills his heart;
The drops are infinite that make a flood,
And yet thou know'st we call it but a rain. 60
There is but one France, one king of France;
That France hath no more kings, and that same king
Hath but the puissant legion of one king,

And we have one; then apprehend no odds,
For one to one is fair equality.   65

Enter a herald from King John

What tidings, messenger, be plain and brief.

Herald   The king of France, my sovereign lord and master,
                Greets by me his foe, the Prince of Wales.
                If thou call forth a hundred men of name,
                Of lords, knights, squires and English gentlemen,   70
                And with thyself and those kneel at his feet,
                He straight will fold his bloody colours up,
                And ransom shall redeem lives forfeited;
                If not, this day shall drink more English blood
                Than ere was buried in our Breton earth.   75
                What is the answer to his proffered mercy?

Prince   This heaven that covers France contains the mercy
                That draws from me submissive orisons;
                That such base breath should vanish from my lips
                To urge the plea of mercy to a man   80
                The Lord forbid; return and tell thy king
                My tongue is made of steel, and it shall beg
                My mercy on his coward burgonet.
                Tell him my colours are as red as his,
                My men as bold, our English arms as strong,   85
                Return him my defiance in his face.

Herald   I go.   *Exit*

Enter another herald

Prince   What news with thee?

2 Herald   The Duke of Normandy, my lord and master,
                Pitying thy youth is so engirt with peril,
                By me hath sent a nimble-jointed jennet,   90
                As swift as ever yet thou didst bestride,
                And therewithal he counsels thee to fly,
                Else death himself hath sworn that thou shalt die.

Prince	Back with the beast unto the beast that sent him.
	Tell him I cannot sit a coward's horse. 95
	Bid him today bestride the jade himself,
	For I will stain my horse quite o'er with blood,
	And double gild my spurs, but I will catch him.
	So tell the cap'ring boy, and get thee gone. *Exit herald*

Enter another herald

3 Herald	Edward of Wales, Philip the second son 100
	To the most mighty Christian King of France,
	Seeing thy body's living date expired,
	All full of charity and Christian love,
	Commends this book full fraught with prayers
	To thy fair hand, and for thy hour of life, 105
	Entreats thee that thou meditate therein,
	And arm thy soul for her long journey towards.
	Thus have I done his bidding, and return.
Prince	Herald of Philip, greet thy lord from me.
	All good that he can send I can receive, 110
	But think'st thou not the unadvisèd boy
	Hath wronged himself in thus far tendering me?
	Haply he cannot pray without the book;
	I think him no divine extemporal.
	Then render back this commonplace of prayer, 115
	To do himself good in adversity.
	Besides, he knows not my sins' quality,
	And therefore knows no prayers for my avail.
	Ere night his prayer may be to pray to God,
	To put it in my heart to hear his prayer. 120
	So tell the courtly wanton, and be gone.
3 Herald	I go. *Exit*
Prince	How confident their strength and number makes them.
	Now Audley, sound those silver wings of thine,
	And let those milk-white messengers of time 125
	Show thy time's learning in this dangerous time.

Thyself art busy and bit with many broils,
And stratagems forepast with iron pens
Are texted in thine honourable face.
Thou art a married man in this distress,   130
But danger woos me as a blushing maid.
Teach me an answer to this perilous time.

Audley   To die is all as common as to live;
The one in choice the other holds in chase,
For from the instant we begin to live,   135
We do pursue and hunt the time to die.
First bud we, then we blow, and after seed,
Then presently we fall, and as a shade
Follows the body, so we follow death.
If then we hunt for death, why do we fear it?   140
If we fear it, why do we follow it?
If we do follow it, how can we shun it?
If we do fear, with fear we do but aid
The thing we fear to seize on us the sooner.
If we fear not, then no resolvèd proffer,   145
Can overthrow the limit of our fate,
For whether ripe or rotten, drop we shall,
As we do draw the lottery of our doom.

Prince   Ah good old man, a thousand thousand armours
These words of thine have buckled on my back,   150
Ah what an idiot hast thou made of life,
To seek the thing it fears, and how disgraced
The imperial victory of murd'ring death,
Since all the lives his conquering arrows strike
Seek him, and he not them, to shame his glory.   155
I will not give a penny for a life,
Nor half a halfpenny to shun grim death,
Since for to live is but to seek to die,
And dying but beginning of new life.
Let come the hour when he that rules it will,   160
To live or die I hold indifferent.   *Exeunt*

SCENE THIRTEEN

Enter King John and Charles

King John   A sudden darkness hath defaced the sky,
The winds are crept into their caves for fear,
The leaves move not, the world is hushed and still,
The birds cease singing, and the wand'ring brooks,
Murmur no wonted greeting to their shores;   5
Silence attends some wonder, and expecteth
That heaven should pronounce some prophecy.
Where or from whom proceeds this silence, Charles?

Charles   Our men with open mouths and staring eyes
Look on each other, as they did attend   10
Each other's words, and yet no creature speaks;
A tongue-tied fear hath made a midnight hour,
And speeches sleep through all the waking regions.

King John   But now the pompous sun in all his pride
Looked through his golden coach upon the world,   15
And on a sudden hath he hid himself,
That now the under earth is as a grave,
Dark, deadly, silent, and uncomfortable.

A clamour of ravens

Hark, what a deadly outcry do I hear?

Enter Philip

Charles   Here comes my brother Philip.

King John   All dismayed.   20
What fearful words are those thy looks presage?

Philip   A flight, a flight –

King John   Coward, what flight? Thou liest, there needs no flight.

Philip   A flight –

King John   Awake thy craven powers, and tell on   25
The substance of that very fear indeed
Which is so ghastly printed in thy face.
What is the matter?

Philip   A flight of ugly ravens
Do croak and hover o'er our soldiers' heads
And keep in triangles and cornered squares,   30
Right as our forces are embattlèd;
With their approach there came this sudden fog,
Which now hath hid the airy floor of heaven,
And made at noon a night unnatural,
Upon the quaking and dismayèd world.   35
In brief, our soldiers have let fall their arms,
And stand like metamorphosed images,
Bloodless and pale, one gazing on another.

King John   Ay, now I call to mind the prophecy,
But I must give no entrance to a fear.   40
Return and hearten up those yielding souls,
Tell them the ravens, seeing them in arms,
So many fair against a famished few,
Come but to dine upon their handiwork,
And prey upon the carrion that they kill;   45
For when we see a horse laid down to die,
Although not dead, the ravenous birds
Sit watching the departure of his life:
Even so these ravens for the carcasses
Of those poor English that are marked to die   50
Hover about, and if they cry to us,
'Tis but for meat that we must kill for them.
Away and comfort up my soldiers,
And sound the trumpets, and at once dispatch
This little business of a silly fraud.   55

                                  Exit Philip

Another noise. Salisbury brought in by a French Captain

Captain	Behold my liege, this knight and forty more,
	Of whom the better part are slain and fled,
	With all endeavour sought to break our ranks,
	And make their way to the encompassed prince.
	Dispose of him as please your majesty.

60

King John	Go, and the next bough, soldier, that thou seest,
	Disgrace it with his body presently,
	For I do hold a tree in France too good
	To be the gallows of an English thief.

Salisbury	My Lord of Normandy, I have your pass

65

	And warrant for my safety through this land.

Charles	Villiers procured it for thee, did he not?

Salisbury	He did.

Charles	And it is current, thou shalt freely pass.

King John	Ay, freely to the gallows to be hanged,

70

	Without denial or impediment.
	Away with him.

Charles	I hope your highness will not so disgrace me,
	And dash the virtue of my seal at arms.
	He hath my never broken name to show,

75

	Charactered with this princely hand of mine,
	And rather let me leave to be a prince
	Than break the stable verdict of a prince.
	I do beseech you let him pass in quiet.

King John	Thou and thy word lie both in my command.

80

	What canst thou promise that I cannot break?
	Which of these twain is greater infamy,
	To disobey thy father or thyself?
	Thy word nor no man's may exceed his power,
	Nor that same man doth never break his word

85

That keeps it to the utmost of his power.
The breach of faith dwells in the soul's consent,
Which if thyself without consent do break,
Thou art not chargèd with the breach of faith.
Go hang him, for thy licence lies in me,   90
And my constraint stands the excuse for thee.

Charles   What, am I not a soldier in my word?
Then arms adieu, and let them fight that list.
Shall I not give my girdle from my waist,
But with a guardian I shall be controlled,   95
To say I may not give my things away?
Upon my soul, had Edward Prince of Wales
Engaged his word, writ down his noble hand,
For all your knights to pass his father's land,
The royal king, to grace his warlike son,   100
Would not alone safe conduct give to them,
But with all bounty feasted them and theirs.

King John   Dwell'st thou on precedents? Then be it so.
Say, Englishman, of what degree thou art.

Salisbury   An earl in England, though a prisoner here,   105
And those that know me call me Salisbury.

King John   Then Salisbury, say whither thou art bound.

Salisbury   To Calais, where my liege king Edward is.

King John   To Calais, Salisbury? Then to Calais pack,
And bid the king prepare a noble grave   110
To put his princely son black Edward in.
And as thou travell'st westward from this place,
Some two leagues hence there is a lofty hill
Whose top seems topless, for the embracing sky
Doth hide his high head in her azure bosom,   115
Upon whose tall top when thy foot attains,
Look back upon the humble vale beneath,
Humble of late, but now made proud with arms,

And thence behold the wretched Prince of Wales,
Hooped with a bond of iron round about;   120
After which sight to Calais spur amain,
And say the prince was smothered, and not slain,
And tell the king this is not all his ill,
For I will greet him ere he thinks I will.
Away be gone, the smoke but of our shot   125
Will choke our foes, though bullets hit them not.

Exeunt

SCENE FOURTEEN

Alarum. Enter Prince Edward and Artois

Artois   How fares your grace, are you not shot my lord?

Prince   No dear Artois, but choked with dust and smoke,
And stepped aside for breath and fresher air.

Artois   Breathe then, and to it again; the amazèd French
Are quite distract with gazing on the crows,   5
And were our quivers full of shafts again,
Your grace should see a glorious day of this.
O for more arrows, Lord, that's our want.

Prince   Courage Artois, a fig for feathered shafts,
When feathered fowls do bandy on our side.   10
What need we fight and sweat and keep a coil,
When railing crows outscold our adversaries?
Up, up, Artois, the ground itself is armed
With fire-containing flint; command our bows
To hurl away their pretty-coloured yew,   15
And to it with stones. Away Artois, away,
My soul doth prophesy we win the day.

Exeunt

Alarum. Enter King John

King John   Our multitudes are in themselves confounded,
Dismayèd and distraught; swift-starting fear
Hath buzzed a cold dismay through all our army,   20
And every petty disadvantage prompts
The fear-possessèd abject soul to fly.
Myself whose spirit is steel to their dull lead,

What with recalling of the prophecy,
And that our native stones from English arms   25
Rebel against us, find myself attainted
With strong surprise of weak and yielding fear.

Enter Charles

Charles   Fly father, fly, the French do kill the French,
Some that would stand let drive at some that fly,
Our drums strike nothing but discouragement,   30
Our trumpets sound dishonour and retire;
The spirit of fear that feareth naught but death,
Cowardly works confusion on itself.

Enter Philip

Philip   Pluck out your eyes, and see not this day's shame.
An arm hath beat an army, one poor David   35
Hath with a stone foiled twenty stout Goliaths.
Some twenty naked starvelings with small flints
Hath driven back a puissant host of men,
Arrayed and fenced in all accomplements.

King John   *Mort Dieu*, they quoit at us, and kill us up.   40
No less than forty thousand wicked elders
Have forty lean slaves this day stoned to death.

Charles   O that I were some other countryman!
This day hath set derision on the French,
And all the world will blurt and scorn at us.   45

King John   What, is there no hope left?

Philip   No hope but death to bury up our shame.

King John   Make up once more with me, the twentieth part
Of those that live are men enough to quail
The feeble handful on the adverse part.   50

Charles   Then charge again. If heaven be not opposed
We cannot lose the day.

King John   On, away.

Exeunt

Enter Audley wounded, and rescued by two squires

1 Squire   How fares my lord?

Audley   Even as a man may do
              That dines at such a bloody feast as this.

2 Squire   I hope, my lord, that is no mortal scar.   55

Audley   No matter if it be, the count is cast,
              And in the worst ends but a mortal man.
              Good friends convey me to the princely Edward,
              That in the crimson bravery of my blood
              I may become him with saluting him.   60
              I'll smile and tell him that this open scar
              Doth end the harvest of his Audley's war.

Exeunt

SCENE FIFTEEN

Enter Prince Edward, King John, Charles,
and all, with ensigns spread. Retreat sounded

Prince   Now John in France, and lately John of France,
Thy bloody ensigns are my captive colours,
And you, high-vaunting Charles of Normandy,
That once today sent me a horse to fly,
Are now the subjects of my clemency.   5
Fie lords, is it not a shame that English boys,
Whose early days are yet not worth a beard,
Should in the bosom of your kingdom thus,
One against twenty beat you up together?

King John   Thy fortune, not thy force, hath conquered us.   10

Prince   An argument that heaven aids the right.

Enter Artois and Philip

See, see, Artois doth bring with him along
The late good counsel-giver to my soul.
Welcome Artois, and welcome Philip too.
Who now of you or I have need to pray?   15
Now is the proverb verified in you,
Too bright a morning breeds a louring day.

Sound trumpets. Enter Audley

But say, what grim discouragement comes here?
Alas, what thousand armèd men of France
Have writ that note of death in Audley's face?   20
Speak thou, that wooest death with thy careless smile
And look'st so merrily upon thy grave

As if thou wert enamoured on thine end,
What hungry sword hath so bereaved thy face,
And lopped a true friend from my loving soul?   25

Audley   O Prince, thy sweet bemoaning speech to me
Is as a mournful knell to one dead sick.

Prince   Dear Audley, if my tongue ring out thy end,
My arms shall be thy grave. What may I do,
To win thy life, or to revenge thy death?   30
If thou wilt drink the blood of captive kings,
Or that it were restorative, command
A health of kings' blood, and I'll drink to thee.
If honour may dispense for thee with death,
The never-dying honour of this day   35
Share wholly, Audley, to thyself and live.

Audley   Victorious Prince – that thou art so, behold
A Caesar's fame in kings' captivity –
If I could hold dim death but at a bay
Till I did see my liege thy royal father,   40
My soul should yield this castle of my flesh,
This mangled tribute, with all willingness
To darkness, consummation, dust and worms.

Prince   Cheerily bold man, thy soul is all too proud
To yield her city for one little breach,   45
Should be divorcèd from her earthly spouse
By the soft temper of a Frenchman's sword.
Lo, to repair thy life I give to thee,
Three thousand marks a year in English land.

Audley   I take thy gift to pay the debts I owe.   50
These two poor squires redeemed me from the French
With lusty and dear hazard of their lives;
What thou hast given me I give to them,
And as thou lov'st me, Prince, lay thy consent
To this bequeath in my last testament.   55

Prince   Renownèd Audley, live and have from me,
          This gift twice doubled to these squires and thee.
          But live or die, what thou hast given away,
          To these and theirs shall lasting freedom stay.
          Come gentlemen, I'll see my friend bestowed   60
          Within an easy litter, then we'll march
          Proudly toward Calais with triumphant pace,
          Unto my royal father, and there bring
          The tribute of my wars, fair France his king.

                                                   Exeunt

SCENE SIXTEEN

Enter six citizens in their shirts, barefoot, with halters about their necks.
Enter King Edward, Queen Philippe, Derby, and soldiers

King   No more Queen Philippe, pacify yourself.
Copland, except he can excuse his fault,
Shall find displeasure written in our looks.
And now unto this proud resisting town:
Soldiers assault, I will no longer stay,   5
To be deluded by their false delays.
Put all to sword, and make the spoil your own.

All Citizens Mercy King Edward, mercy gracious lord.

King   Contemptuous villains, call ye now for truce?
Mine ears are stopped against your bootless cries,   10
Sound drums alarum, draw threat'ning swords.

1 Citizen Ah noble prince, take pity on this town,
And hear us, mighty King:
We claim the promise that your highness made:
The two days' respite is not yet expired,   15
And we are come with willingness to bear
What torturing death or punishment you please,
So that the trembling multitude be saved.

King   My promise? Well I do confess as much;
But I require the chiefest citizens,   20
And men of most account that should submit.
You peradventure are but servile grooms,
Or some felonious robbers on the sea,
Whom apprehended law would execute,
Albeit severity lay dead in us.   25
No no, ye cannot overreach us thus.

2 Citizen	The sun, dread lord, that in the western fall,
	Beholds us now low brought through misery,
	Did in the orient purple of the morn
	Salute our coming forth when we were known, 30
	Or may our portion be with damnèd fiends.
King	If it be so, then let our covenant stand;
	We take possession of the town in peace.
	But for yourselves, look you for no remorse,
	But as imperial justice hath decreed, 35
	Your bodies shall be dragged about these walls,
	And after feel the stroke of quartering steel.
	This is your doom, go soldiers, see it done.
Queen	Ah be more mild unto these yielding men.
	It is a glorious thing to 'stablish peace, 40
	And kings approach the nearest unto God,
	By giving life and safety unto men.
	As thou intendest to be king of France,
	So let her people live to call thee king,
	For what the sword cuts down or fire hath spoiled 45
	Is held in reputation none of ours.
King	Although experience teach us this is true,
	That peaceful quietness brings most delight
	When most of all abuses are controlled,
	Yet insomuch it shall be known that we 50
	As well can master our affections
	As conquer other by the dint of sword,
	Philippe prevail, we yield to thy request,
	These men shall live to boast of clemency,
	And Tyranny, strike terror to thyself. 55
2 Citizen	Long live your highness, happy be your reign.
King	Go get you hence, return unto the town,
	And if this kindness hath deserved your love,
	Learn then to reverence Edward as your king.

Exeunt Citizens

Now might we hear of our affairs abroad,   60
We would till gloomy winter were o'erspent,
Dispose our men in garrison a while.
But who comes here?

Enter Copland and King David

Derby   Copland my lord, and David King of Scots.

King   Is this the proud presumptuous esquire of the north,   65
             That would not yield his prisoner to my Queen?

Copland   I am my liege a northern squire indeed,
             But neither proud nor insolent, I trust.

King   What moved thee then to be so obstinate
             To contradict our royal Queen's desire?   70

Copland   No wilful disobedience, mighty lord,
             But my desert and public law of arms.
             I took the king myself in single fight,
             And like a soldier would be loath to lose
             The least pre-eminence that I had won.   75
             And Copland straight upon your highness' charge
             Is come to France, and with a lowly mind
             Doth vail the bonnet of his victory:
             Receive, dread lord, the custom of my freight,
             The wealthy tribute of my labouring hands,   80
             Which should long since have been surrendered up
             Had but your gracious self been there in place.

Queen   But Copland, thou didst scorn the King's command,
             Neglecting our commission in his name.

Copland   His name I reverence, but his person more.   85
             His name shall keep me in allegiance still,
             But to his person I will bend my knee.

King   I pray thee, Philippe, let displeasure pass:
             This man doth please me, and I like his words,

For what is he that will attempt great deeds,   90
And lose the glory that ensues the same?
All rivers have recourse unto the sea,
And Copland's faith relation to his king.
Kneel therefore down. Now rise King Edward's knight,
And to maintain thy state I freely give   95
Five hundred marks a year to thee and thine.

Enter Salisbury

Welcome lord Salisbury, what news from Brittany?

Salisbury   This, mighty King: the country we have won,
And Charles de Montfort, regent of that place,
Presents your highness with this coronet,   100
Protesting true allegiance to your grace.

King   We thank thee for thy service, valiant earl.
Challenge our favour, for we owe it thee.

Salisbury   But now my lord, as this is joyful news,
So must my voice be tragical again,   105
And I must sing of doleful accidents.

King   What, have our men the overthrow at Poitiers,
Or is our son beset with too much odds?

Salisbury   He was my lord, and as my worthless self,
With forty other serviceable knights,   110
Under safe conduct of the dauphin's seal,
Did travel that way, finding him distressed,
A troop of lances met us on the way,
Surprised and brought us prisoners to the king,
Who proud of this, and eager of revenge,   115
Commanded straight to cut off all our heads,
And surely we had died but that the Duke,
More full of honour than his angry sire,
Procured our quick deliverance from thence.
But ere we went, 'Salute your king', quoth he,   120

'Bid him provide a funeral for his son;
Today our sword shall cut his thread of life,
And sooner than he thinks we'll be with him,
To quittance those displeasures he hath done.'
This said, we passed, not daring to reply;   125
Our hearts were dead, our looks diffused and wan.
Wandering at last we climbed unto a hill,
From whence, although our grief were much before,
Yet now to see the occasion with our eyes
Did thrice so much increase our heaviness,   130
For there my lord, oh there we did descry
Down in a valley how both armies lay:
The French had cast their trenches like a ring,
And every barricado's open front
Was thick embossed with brazen ordinance.   135
Here stood a battle of ten thousand horse,
There twice as many pikes in quadrant wise,
Here crossbows and deadly wounding darts,
And in the midst, like to a slender point
Within the compass of the horizon,   140
As 'twere a rising bubble in the sea,
A hazel wand amidst a wood of pines,
Or as a bear fast chained unto a stake,
Stood famous Edward, still expecting when
Those dogs of France would fasten on his flesh.   145
Anon the death-procuring knell begins,
Off go the canons that with trembling noise
Did shake the very mountain where they stood,
Then sound the trumpets' clangour in the air,
The battles join, and when we could no more   150
Discern the difference 'twixt the friend and foe,
So intricate the dark confusion was,
Away we turned our wat'ry eyes with sighs,
As black as powder fuming into smoke.
And thus I fear, unhappy, have I told,   155
The most untimely tale of Edward's fall.

Queen	Ah me, is this my welcome into France?
	Is this the comfort that I looked to have,
	When I should meet with my belovèd son?
	Sweet Ned, I would thy mother in the sea 160
	Had been prevented of this mortal grief.
King	Content thee Philippe, 'tis not tears will serve
	To call him back, if he be taken hence.
	Comfort thyself as I do, gentle Queen,
	With hope of sharp unheard-of dire revenge. 165
	He bids me to provide his funeral,
	And so I will, but all the peers in France
	Shall mourners be, and weep out bloody tears,
	Until their empty veins be dry and sere.
	The pillars of his hearse shall be their bones, 170
	The mould that covers him, their city ashes,
	His knell the groaning cries of dying men,
	And in the stead of tapers on his tomb
	An hundred fifty towers shall burning blaze,
	While we bewail our valiant son's decease. 175

After a flourish sounded within, enter a herald

Herald	Rejoice my lord, ascend the imperial throne.
	The mighty and redoubted Prince of Wales,
	Great servitor to bloody Mars in arms,
	The Frenchman's terror and his country's fame,
	Triumphant rideth like a Roman peer, 180
	And lowly at his stirrup comes afoot
	King John of France, together with his son,
	In captive bonds, whose diadem he brings
	To crown thee with, and to proclaim thee king.
King	Away with mourning, Philippe, wipe thine eyes. 185
	Sound trumpets, welcome in Plantagenet.

Enter Prince Edward, King John, Phillip,
Audley, and Artois

As things long lost when they are found again,
So doth my son rejoice his father's heart,
For whom even now my soul was much perplexed.

Queen   Be this a token to express my joy (*kisses him*),   190
            For inward passions will not let me speak.

Prince   My gracious father, here receive the gift,
            This wreath of conquest, and reward of war,
            Got with as mickle peril of our lives,
            As ere was thing of price before this day.   195
            Install your highness in your proper right,
            And herewithal I render to your hands
            These prisoners, chief occasion of our strife.

King   So John of France, I see you keep your word.
            You promised to be sooner with ourself   200
            Than we did think for, and 'tis so indeed.
            But had you done at first as now you do,
            How many civil towns had stood untouched
            That now are turned to ragged heaps of stone,
            How many people's lives mightst thou have saved   205
            That are untimely sunk into their graves!

King John   Edward, recount not things irrevocable,
            Tell me what ransom thou requir'st to have.

King   Thy ransom, John, hereafter shall be known.
            But first to England thou must cross the seas,   210
            To see what entertainment it affords.
            Howe'er it falls, it cannot be so bad
            As ours hath been since we arrived in France.

King John   Accursèd man, of this I was foretold,
            But did misconster what the prophet told.   215

Prince   Now father, this petition Edward makes
            To thee whose grace hath been his strongest shield:
            That as thy pleasure chose me for the man

To be the instrument to show thy power,
So thou wilt grant that many princes more,   220
Bred and brought up within that little isle,
May still be famous for like victories;
And for my part, the bloody scars I bear,
The weary nights that I have watched in field,
The dangerous conflicts I have often had,   225
The fearful menaces were proffered me,
The heat and cold, and what else might displease,
I wish were now redoubled twenty fold,
So that hereafter ages when they read
The painful traffic of my tender youth   230
Might thereby be inflamed with such resolve
As not the territories of France alone,
But likewise Spain, Turkey, and what countries else
That justly would provoke fair England's ire,
Might at their presence tremble and retire.   235

King   Here, English lords, we do proclaim a rest,
         An intercession of our painful arms.
         Sheathe up your swords, refresh your weary limbs,
         Peruse your spoils, and after we have breathed
         A day or two within this haven town,   240
         God willing then for England we'll be shipped,
         Where in a happy hour I trust we shall
         Arrive three kings, two princes, and a queen.
                                                     Exeunt

                    F I N I S